THE
WHITE FLAG
PRINCIPLE

THE
WHITE FLAG
PRINCIPLE

How to Lose
a War and Why

Shimon Tzabar

FOUR WALLS EIGHT WINDOWS
NEW YORK

Copyright © 1972, 2002 Shimon Tzabar

Published by
Four Walls Eight Windows
39 West 14th Street
New York, NY 10011

http://www.4w8w.com

First published in 1972.

Library of Congress Cataloguing-in-Publication Data:

Tzabar, Shimon, 1926–
    The white flag principle: how to lose a war and why / Shimon Tzabar.
        p.   cm.
    Includes bibliographical references.
    ISBN: 1-56858-259-5 (pbk.)
    1. War. I. Title.
U21.5.T98 2003
355.02—dc21   20020044788

10   9   8   7   6   5   4   3   2   1

Printed in Canada

Caveat

Although the author and the publishers have full confidence in the negative value of *The White Flag Principle*, they reserve their right to reject any claim for damages or compensation resulting from correct or incorrect use of any of the tips, ideas, recommendations and directions expressed in or derived from *The White Flag Principle* which may result in victory.

Contents

ONE

Why Defeat?

WAR WAS, AND STILL IS, the most important event in the history of mankind. It is the womb that bears fortunes and misfortunes, hopes and disappointments, life and death. It creates and destroys tribes, nations, kingdoms and empires. "War is the father of all things," said Heraclitus.

It is not surprising that the human mind is so obsessed by war. Reflections of this obsession find their way into every human activity—into philosophy, into the arts, into science, into social structures and political organizations.[1] The concept of war dominates the human mind to such an extent that "the dualism that characterized the traditional dialectic of all branches of philosophy and of stable political relationships stems from war as the prototype of conflict. Except for secondary considerations, there cannot be, to put it as simply as possible, more than two sides to a question, because there cannot be more than two sides to a war."[2] The best brains have tried to understand war; to study it, analyze and inspect it in order to discover the rules by which it operates. However, war has been studied not just for the sake of knowledge, but for the sake of victory. The study of war has been for the most part the search for the key to victory. Nothing else has been held important or even significant. The blood, the fire, the pain and the misery have not just been ignored; they have been justified and glorified because, if manipulated properly, they have led to victory. "Victory at all costs," said Churchill, "victory in spite of all terror, victory however long and hard the road may be; for without victory there is no survival."[3]

What Churchill said to one people about one particular war has been true for all wars and for all combatants. Victory was the ultimate goal, shared historically and psychologically by all members of the human species. "Military glory! It was a dream that century after century had seized on men's imaginations and set their blood on fire. Trumpets, plumes, charges, the pomp of war, the excitement of combat, the exultation of victory—the mixture was intoxicating indeed. To command great armies, to perform deeds of valor, to ride victorious through flower-strewn streets, to be heroic, magnificent, famous—such were the visions that danced before men's eyes as they turned eagerly to war."[4]

The desire to be victorious was so elementary and obvious that when von Clausewitz wrote a classic on the subject, he called it *On War*. A more accurate title would have been *On Victory*. He assumed automatically that the two were coterminous, indeed identical.

Are they really identical?

War can be described as a one-dimensional process in time.[5] It is preceded by a prewar situation and followed by a postwar situation. On paper, this can be represented as three lines, one preceding the other:

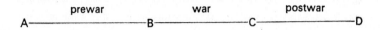

Since the outcome of war—victory or defeat—provides for different postwar situations, it is better to draw the diagram in two dimensions rather than in one.

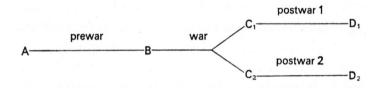

We have two possible outcomes of war (C_1, C_2) and two possible postwar situations (C_1-D_1, C_2-D_2). The outcomes are defeat and victory; the postwar situations are good and bad. It is taken for granted that a good postwar situation is the result of victory, the bad the result of defeat. This might be true if the factors that lead an army to victory were the same as those that create a better postwar situation. As it is, the factors are not the same, and it does not necessarily follow that victory results in a good postwar situation and defeat in a bad one.

Germany and Japan, the most heavily defeated parties in the last world war, emerged better off and had a much better postwar situation than Britain and France, the victorious parties. The same is true of modern China, which has been defeated continually in the last few hundred years, and of Russia, which suffered perpetual defeats from the beginning of the twentieth century to 1942, when the invading German army started to collapse under the weight of its own victories.

The advantages of defeat are many. They can be cultural, social, economic and even military. When the Second World War broke out, Japan was a socioeconomic monster—a hybrid of a feudal society and a modern economy. If Japan had won the war, this monster would have grown bigger. In the end, it would have destroyed its people. Since the monster was a result of one thousand years of continual victories, it could be destroyed only by defeat. Two atom bombs—one on Hiroshima and one on Nagasaki—did it. The defeat delivered Japan from its abnormality. It had a beneficial effect on the economy, on the social life, on the arts, on everything.

Similar things can be said about Germany. Her triumph during the French financial crisis of November, 1968, when the economy and the monetary system of the Western world depended on the Deutschmark, was but the peak of an unbroken range of economic miracles. This was only one of the many advantages the Germans derived from their defeat. If Germany had been victorious, the Germans would have had to carry on under the Nazi yoke of Hitler and his gang, which would have been fatal to Germany no less than to the rest of the world. If Germany had won, the economic miracle would have been impossible. If the Germans had won, they would have had to keep their army in distant foreign countries and pay for the upkeep of that army with their economic progress. In short, they would have had to suffer what France and Britain, the victors, have suffered in the last twenty-five years.

And who is more experienced in defeat than the Jewish people? They have been the world's professional vanquished for almost two thousand years. It is hardly possible to mention a defeat, a surrender or a *débâcle* which they have not suffered. And yet they have survived all their victors. Where are the ancient kingdoms that destroyed Israel? Where are the Egyptians and the Babylonians, where are the Greeks, where are the Romans who burned down their temple? They are all dead now, vanished from the political map. It is the defeated Jews who are still here with enough vigor in their old bones to start afresh from the beginning.

The view that the best outcome of war can only be the result of victory has been common. Nevertheless, there have been a few who suspected that it might not be so.

The best known example is that of King Pyrrhus, who said to his friends when they congratulated him on his victory over the Romans: "Yes, but if we have another victory, we are undone!" A similar idea was expressed by Belisarius while defending and expanding Justinian's empire. When his soldiers urged him to attack the king of the Saracens, who was moving along the Euphrates with the aim of pouncing upon Antioch, he answered: "True victory lies in compelling one's opponent to abandon his purpose with the least possible loss to oneself. If such a result was obtained, there was no real advantage to be gained by winning a battle."[6] Samuel Rogers quotes the Duke of Wellington as saying after Waterloo: "The next greatest misfortune to losing a battle is to gain such a victory as this."[7]

The quotations from King Pyrrhus and the Duke of Wellington express a surprise that experience does not tally with what is commonly believed as true. Belisarius' answer shows more than that. It shows that this outstanding general realized that victory is not at all necessary for the achievement of aims.

In our own times, this approach was followed by the noted exponent of the indirect approach in strategy, Captain B. H. Liddell Hart. He was unique in the military profession in that he questioned the role of victory on the battlefield. "The object in war," wrote Liddell Hart, "is a better state of peace—even if only from your point of view. Hence it is essential to conduct war with constant regard to the peace you desire.

History shows that gaining military victory is not in itself equivalent to gaining the object of policy. But as most of the thinking about war has been done by the military profession, there has been a very natural tendency to lose sight of the basic national object and to identify it with the military aim."[8]

It was natural for the exponent of the indirect approach to recommend an indirect victory. But it was a victory nevertheless. A different opinion altogether, challenging victory itself, was put forward by Professor Anatol Rapoport:

> The victorious wars of Napoleon, the German victories of 1864, 1866 and 1870 and the triumph of Japan over China (1895) and over Russia (1905), were only episodes presaging the eventual defeat of France, Germany and Japan. If, then, we extend von Clausewitz's dictum that only the outcome of the final war counts in the career of a war-waging state, we must conclude on the basis of historical experience that military prowess is more likely to lead to defeat than to victory.[9]

Rapoport knows more about victory than the most distinguished generals. However, he does not draw any conclusions. He does not make the necessary step of relating victory—as he understands it—to the real aim of war. This missing link in the otherwise logical chain of thought has been provided not by historians, soldiers or politicians, but by men of letters. "Misery me!" cried Bilbo Baggins. "I have heard songs of many battles, and I always understood that defeat may be glorious."[10] Another writer, Joseph Heller, states this more explicitly:

You put so much stock in *winning* wars . . . The real trick lies in *losing* wars, in knowing which wars can be *lost*. Italy has been losing wars for centuries, and just see how splendidly we've done nonetheless. France wins wars and is in a continual state of crisis. Germany loses and prospers . . . Italy won a war in Ethiopia and promptly stumbled into serious trouble. Victory gave us such insane delusions of grandeur that we helped start a world war we hadn't a chance of winning. But now that we are losing again, everything has taken a turn for the better, and we will certainly come out on top again if we succeed in being defeated.[11]

Some have been suspicious of the alleged positive effect of victory. Others have been aware of the superiority of defeat. Nobody, however, has tried to put into practice this unconventional but more realistic approach. When we watch the huge professional armies with their incredible firepower, with their scientists, with their electronic computers and with the synthetic rationalism of their Herman Kahns, this neglect seems almost unbelievable. Fortunately, this is now corrected with the publication of *The White Flag Principle*.

What Is *The White Flag Principle*?

If we agree that a military disaster may produce a better postwar situation than victory, then there should be a science of military disasters as there is a science of military victories. Such a science must comprise a theory and a practice. The practice should provide armies with handbooks and textbooks for the accomplishment of defeats and surrenders. The sole remaining superpower, the United States, is so powerful that it renders absurd any effort by lesser powers to overcome it in the traditional way. This fact makes an alternative to victory even more urgent.

Let us take, for example, a political conflict like the 1968 invasion of Czechoslovakia by the Soviet Union, which was still a superpower at that time. The discrepancy in power between the two forces was so great that the Czechs had to revert to the only stratagem left to them—namely, that of surrender. The Czechs are almost experts in the art of submission. They sabotaged the war machine of the Austro-Hungarian empire in the First World War by similar methods; as a result, they won an independent state of Czechoslovakia. While others rebelled, killed and were killed, the Czechs won independence by conforming to every rule and law, however stupid and ridiculous. Readers interested in details should read *The Good Soldier Schweik*, by Jaroslav Hašek. Though written as literary fiction, it is a practical manual of how to produce military disasters.

The outcome of the Czechs' surrender to the Russian invasion of 1968 was that they were made a better offer than were the Hungarians after their bloody revolt of 1956. Moreover, the Soviet Union, with all its might, with all its A- and H-bombs and with all its intercontinental missiles, had to withdraw most of its forces with almost no shots fired. Emil Zatopek, the famous Czech sportsman, was quoted in the British press as saying: "The Russians came crashing here stupidly, with none of the gentle movement of sportsmen. They came with all their armaments and their might, but were defeated by our children with nothing but flags on their chest and the power of their words to unite our people."[12]

Even if the superiority of defeat over victory will be accepted, people could still argue that, once we have grasped the idea, a handbook for defeat is unnecessary because it is easy to lose a war, and that all one has to do in order to be defeated is to handle the war in an inefficient manner. It is easy to show that this is an impractical approach. If "inefficient manner" means the handling of a war not in the way it is taught in the military academies, then we will be surprised to learn how many wars have been won in this way. Colonel Alfred H. Burne, in a textbook for winning wars which is much in use in military institutions around the world, admits that some generals have won battles in spite of transgressing or by ignoring one or more of these "principles of war, while other generals appear to have observed them and yet have suffered defeat."[13] No one can lose a war by handling it inefficiently any more than one can win by handling it efficiently. This is so, not because there are no rules in warfare, but because of two elements in war that cannot be predicted: *chance* and *friction*.[14] Friction and chance make perfection in fighting impossible. Wars have been won despite imperfections and even despite grave mistakes. This was recognized long ago by the ancient Greeks. "Many badly planned enterprises," says Thucydides in the *History of the Peloponnesian War*, "have had the luck to be successful because the enemy has shown an even smaller degree of intelligence."[15]

Even if war could—theoretically speaking—be handled properly, there is still a need for a manual like *The White Flag Principle*, for the following reasons:

Let us assume for a moment that by handling a war inefficiently, it is possible to lose it. This may have a chance of success if the enemy is stronger than or equal to one's power. If one's enemy is much weaker than oneself, merely pursuing the war in an inefficient manner will not bring about the desired results. The Russians fought the Finns in 1939 in a most inefficient manner and still were unable to lose the war. It may also happen that the enemy, though stronger, had decided to lose. In this case too, not to handle the war in an "efficient manner" will only achieve victory (see Chapter 9).

Mere desire to win has never guaranteed victory; so a desire to lose is not enough to guarantee defeat. For example: it is difficult, almost impossible, to be defeated if one's economy is flourishing. Countries with a strong economy tend to win rather than lose. The same can be said about a strong and united society or a well-balanced and clever foreign policy. To pave the way for a military disaster, one may have to ruin one's own economy (Chapter 4), disunite a united society (Chapter 5) and carry out a bad foreign policy (Chapter 3). All this must be an integral part of *The White Flag Principle*. Even when the war has been eventually lost, some problems still remain unsolved; for example, how to march into captivity and how to face charges as war criminals—a thing quite likely to happen to the vanquished.

In this chapter, which introduces the idea of defeat as the best outcome of war, a brief explanation must be given for the use of a paradoxical term: *power of submission*.

Though the expression "power of submission" may sound like a self-contradiction, this is not so. It is true though that submission, surrender, defeat, *débâcle* and the like, result from lack of power or, more precisely, from lack of *sufficient* power. This applies only to situations in which both opponents fight for victory, each opposing power with power. However, it is possible, as in judo, to oppose power with weakness—that is, to use the enemy's strength to put him out of balance. In this sense, the use of a phrase like "power of submission" is meaningful. When there is a war between two sides and one of them gives himself up, the victor takes full possession of the loser. Since justice, pity, sympathy and love always go to the underdog, the victor has, morally at least, lost. He might even be considered the aggressor (if he was not considered so before). The most evil warmonger has sympathy on his side the moment he loses the battle. Justice is a good argument in war and is used by the belligerent as a sort of weapon. However, the moment the battle is over, it is useless to the victor. He looks ridiculous indeed if he tries to add justice and morals to his power. Israel lost a great deal of world sympathy after her formidable victory over the Arabs in 1967, and her moralistic justifications since then for the occupation of Arab territory have sounded ridiculous, as it sounds now when they bomb the Palestinians in their war against terror.

Once bereft of morality and justice, the victor is vulnerable to all sorts of calamities like corruption, the disillusionment of its young generation, a rapid growth of cultural hypocrisy and so on. Then comes the burden of too many responsibilities. The victor has to take care of his own country and that of his opponent as well. If the burden of ruling one country alone is so heavy as to cause many governments to collapse, the burden of ruling two countries, one of them shattered after a defeat, is not difficult to imagine. The victor has to take care of his opponent's economic situation, of his police, his army, his industry, his education, his foreign affairs, his transport, his everything. The victor can never say, "Sorry, I have troubles of my own." He is the victor, and victory means responsibility. Victors have no choice but to rule and govern. This opens a vast range of possibilities and opportunities for the vanquished. Horace demonstrated a keen sense of observation when he stated that "when Greece had been enslaved [by the Romans] she made a slave of her conqueror and introduced the arts into Latium, which was still rough."[16]

The problems of governing a vanquished enemy are very complicated since they depend to a great extent on future confrontations and future enemies. "Throughout the history of war," says Major General J.F.C. Fuller, "it is noticeable how frequently enemies and friends change sides in rotation. Therefore, once you have knocked your enemy out, it is wise to set him on his feet again, because the chances are that you will need his assistance in the next conflict.[17] As *The White Flag Principle* is not designed to assist the victor, we will not go further into this. We will only point out the difficulties that confront the victors in dealing with their vanquished enemies. The most difficult economic, administrative and sociological tasks and problems have to be carried out and solved by the victor under unfavourable conditions, while the vanquished are free to fend for themselves. A typical example of how happy life is under foreign occupation can be, is shown by the description of Arab life under the Crusaders' occupation in the twelfth century by Ibn Jubayr:

> We left Tibnin by a road flanked throughout its length with farms inhabited by Moslems who lived in great prosperity under the Franks—may Allah preserve us from similar temptation! The conditions imposed on them are the surrender of half their crops at the time of the harvest and the payment of a poll-tax of one dinar seven qirats, as well as a light tax on fruit-trees. The Moslems are masters in their own dwellings and order their affairs as they think best. Such is the constitution of the farms and big villages that they inhabit in the Frankish territory. Many Moslems long in their hearts to settle there, when they see the condition of their brethren in districts under Moslem governments, for the state of these latter is the very opposite of comfortable. It is unfortunate for the Moslems that, in countries governed by their co-religionists, they have always to complain of the injustices of their rulers, whereas they have nothing but praise for the conduct of the Franks, on whose justice they can always rely.[18]

The fate of conquered people should be compared with the fate of free people, and especially of free people belonging to powerful and victorious regimes. In *The Secret History*, Procopius describes the fate of the free citizens of Byzantium under their most glorious ruler, Justinian the Great:

> Without hesitation he [Justinian] issued orders for the seizure of towns, the burning of cities, and the enslavement of entire nations, for no reason at all. So that if one chose to add up all the calamities which have befallen the Romans from the beginning and to weigh them against those for which Justinian was responsible, I feel sure that he would find that a greater slaughter of human beings was brought about by this one man than took place in all the proceeding centuries. As for other people's money, he seized it by stealth without the slightest hesitation; for he did not even think it necessary to put forward any excuse or pretense of justification before taking possession of things to which he had no claim. Yet when he had secured the money he was quite prepared to show his contempt for it by reckless prodigality, or to throw it to potential enemies without the slightest need. In short, he had no money himself and allowed no one else in the world to keep any, as if he were not overcome by avarice but held fast by envy of those who had acquired money. Thus he cheerfully banished wealth from Roman soil and became the creator of nation-wide poverty.[19]

From a purely military point of view, the vanquished are better off than the victors. Guerilla warfare, for example, the only kind of warfare that can challenge the mightiest army, can be used only by the vanquished. It is impossible for a victor to employ guerilla warfare. This is the most ironic consequence of victory.

CASUALTIES IN NAPOLEONIC WARS

Battle	Year	French Casualties	Enemy Casualties
Eylau	1807	22,000	23,000
Wagram	1809	33,000	26,000
Malo Jaroslaw	1812	8,000	8,000
Krasnoi	1812	10,000	5,000
Beresina	1812	10,000	8,000
Lützen	1813	20,000	12,000
Bautzen	1813	21,000	11,000
Katzpach	1813	8,000	4,000

By being victorious, the winner is prevented from using the only kind of warfare that is more powerful than its own. The vanquished are immune not only from guerilla warfare but also from nuclear weapons. They cannot even be threatened by them. An enemy can be threatened with nuclear weapons as long as he is fighting, but the moment he surrenders or has been defeated, he cannot be threatened by anything. Hydrogen bombs and intercontinental missiles become as useless as Stone Age clubs.

There is also a false impression that the vanquished suffer more casualties in war than the victors. Though this may be true of ancient battles, it is certainly not true today. In the battle of Chattanooga, in 1863, the defeated Bragg had only 3,000 casualties against 5,815 casualties of the victorious army of Grant.[21] In the five years of the American Civil War, the victorious North had 334,624 killed and dead from wounds or disease against 192,345 of the vanquished South.[22] Bodart sums up the French casualties in their seven defeats in the Great Turkish War of 1683–99 as being only 43,000, while in their seventeen victories they suffered 50,900.[23] In the War of the Spanish Succession (1701-14), the total French casualties in their victories was 125,700 against 36,700 in their defeats.[24] More impressive is the comparison of casualties in the Napoleonic Wars (see table opposite). Although Napoleon won most of his battles, he paid more for them—as far as casualties are concerned—than his enemies.

However, the balance of corpses was upset once Napoleon started losing. In the battle of Leipzig, when Napoleon was routed, he suffered 50,000 casualties against 75,000 of his opponents, 7,000 against 9,000 in the battle of Paris (1814) and 4,000 against 7,000 in the battle of Toulouse (1814).[25]

In the battle of Port Arthur, in 1905, which opened the bloody wars of the twentieth century, the victorious Japanese sustained 71,000 casualties against 60,000 of the Russians.[26] At the battle of Verdun, in the First World War, the Germans launched a "large scale offensive which began in February 1916. It was marked at first by distinct success, but ultimately resulted in an Allied victory with heavy German losses."[27] What were these "heavy German losses"? The same source, but in another entry, gives the losses of the German army as 427,000 against 535,000 of the victorious French.[28] Taking the result of the whole war into account—not just the results of one isolated battle—we find that the total losses of the belligerents in the First World War are:[29]

The Victors		The Vanquished	
Russia	1,700,000	Germany	1,600,000
France	1,385,000	Austria-Hungary	800,000
Great Britain	900,000	Turkey	250,000
Italy	330,000		
United States	48,900		
Serbia and			
Montenegro	125,000		
Rumania	100,000		
Belgium	102,000		
Bulgaria	100,000		
Greece	7,000		
Portugal	2,000		
Total	4,799,900		2,650,000

Similar results are obtained when we add up all the belligerent losses in the Second World War. These are 14,500,000 for the defeated Axis, 36,236,276 for the victorious Allies.[30]

It is not difficult to explain why the vanquished suffer less than the victorious. A military disaster may be one of two kinds: a defeat or a surrender. In the case of a surrender there is no reason for the vanquished to suffer, since soldiers who surrender are protected by international law and by custom. Soldiers who flee from the battlefield in defeat also have no reason to suffer since they are usually faster than the victors who are pursuing them. Fugitives flee faster because they are less burdened with equipment. They have no booty; even their weapons are often thrown away.[31] The pursuers, on the other hand, have to hold on to their booty and to their weapons. These heavy burdens make them slower in pursuit. (There is a possibility, however, that the vanquished may be utterly liquidated. This happens only in a certain strategical configuration, which is explained in detail in Chapter 7. If the vanquished do not wish their troops to be liquidated, they can avoid such configurations.)

Victors not only suffer greater casualties than the vanquished; they are also more deeply humiliated and degraded. In the nineteenth century, most European generals who were repeatedly defeated by Napoleon managed to remain politically and militarily active and were always able to draft armies for new wars. But for Napoleon, the supreme victor, one defeat was sufficient to send him to Elba and another to end his entire military and political career on St. Helena. Generals who lose are often promoted to higher rank. After his defeat by Frederick the Great in 1757, Prince de Soubise was promoted marshal of France.[32] The Israeli general, Ariel Sharon, who was (despite his victories in the Lebanese war) finally defeated by Hezbollah when he was the defense minister, was not only able to keep his rank and medals when he retired, but was eventually elected prime minister of Israel. Victorious generals, on the other hand, are often dismissed and degraded, as happened to Belisarius or, in more recent times, to Air Chief Marshal Dowding after the Battle of Britain, or to General MacArthur after his victories in Korea.

A more important question has still to be asked: Is defeat superior to victory not only in war (which is only one kind of human conflict) but in conflicts in general? This is a serious question that was partly answered in our explanation of the unparadoxical nature of the term "power of submission" (page 10). However, as *The White Flag Principle* is intended mainly to serve as a manual for war purposes, the more general aspects of the subject are outside the scope of this book.

TWO

Defeat and Victory

In order to be defeated one must be able to distinguish between defeat and victory. Since the two are the outcomes of war, it is also important to know what war is.

There are many definitions of war, ranging from simple and timid ones like "war is a game" to universal ones like that of Heraclitus (see page 1).[33] To start with, let us take the one coined by von Clausewitz, who is most esteemed by the military: "*War is an act of violence intended to compel our opponent to fulfill our will.*"[34] According to this definition, if we succeed in our intention and the enemy submits to our will, we are victorious and our opponent is defeated. What is not so clear is what happens if we do *not* succeed in compelling our enemy to submit to our will. Are we defeated and the enemy victorious, or is it regarded as a stalemate?

Von Clausewitz overcomes this difficulty by assuming that the definition is symmetrical. While we try to compel our opponent to submit to our will, he is trying to compel us to submit to his will. The outcome of war depends on both being belligerent. However, this symmetry is only assumed. It can well happen that the opponent has no intention of making us submit to his will. In such a case, victory or defeat will have no definite meaning.

Suppose that the definition *is* symmetrical. It still does not help us to distinguish between victory and defeat. For example: we declare war; we apply violence to compel our opponent to submit to our will. Our opponent, however, refuses to submit. What are we to do? We can withdraw without being victorious or we can apply more violence. Let us say that we apply more violence. However, our opponent still refuses to surrender. We continue subjecting him to violence until we run out of it. Though we have run out of violence, victory still eludes us because our opponent has not been defeated. *As long as our opponent is not defeated we cannot be victorious!* It can be seen that our victory depends solely on our opponent's surrender, although his surrender does not depend on our victory. An opponent can surrender at any time, with or without our application of violence. "A battle lost," says Ferdinand Foch, "is a battle one thinks one has lost; for a battle cannot be lost physically, it can only be lost morally."[35]

Von Clausewitz was not unaware of the difficulties his definition stumbles into. He tried to circumvent the confusion by making victory independent of the opponent's defeat. He tried to define victory in objective terms. He named three elements that must be found in victory and not in defeat, and then, feeling that these might not be enough, he added a fourth element.

The first three elements of victory—according to von Clausewitz—are: (1) the greater loss of the enemy in physical power, (2) the greater loss of the enemy in moral power, (3) the enemy's avowal of his defeat by the relinquishment of his intentions.[36] The fourth element is the acquisition of trophies: artillery and prisoners.[37]

A few examples can disprove the validity of these elements as objective criteria of victory. The French lost the war in Indochina despite the much greater loss they inflicted on the enemy. The United States forces in Vietnam caused much more physical damage to the North Vietnamese than they suffered themselves, and yet no one dared to call it victory. We will not comment on moral loss, since it is immeasurable, but the third element, "the enemy's avowal of his defeat by the relinquishment of his intentions," is the same as the dependence of victory on the opponent's defeat. Even if it were not so, it still could not be regarded as an objective element of victory since "intentions," "aims" and "goals" tend to change as the fight goes on. Moreover, no commander or politician will declare his true intentions, especially when his intentions are aggressive. The common justification of war is self-defense. Hitler, in a letter to Martin Bormann, declared that the war was forced upon him by the enemies of German National Socialism.[38] The Japanese too stated that their attack on Pearl Harbor was in self-defense.[39] The nature of such a pretext as self-defense is that it cannot be relinquished at any time. We should not overlook the fact that real aims and intentions are part of the *grand strategy* and are always kept secret. It is also unusual to make public the true aims of war, since if they are not achieved there is a loss of face. Statesmen have to be careful not to miss their proclaimed targets. The only way not to miss a target is to shoot first and then draw the bull's-eye around the arrow.

Nor can the last element of victory—trophies of artillery and prisoners—be proof of victory. During the Second World War the

Germans and the Japanese acquired more prisoners, artillery and even territory than the Allies, but victory eluded them.

The problem of telling victory from defeat troubled the ancients no less than it troubles modern armies. Plutarch, for example, thought that the "proof of victory consists in the final mastery of the field, and the side which asks leave evidently does not possess this or else it would take what it wants."[40] The Romans too had difficulty in deciding what victory is. Cicero, in his speech on the command of Cneius Pompeius, complained that "generals have fought against Mithridates in the sort of way which produces the outward signs of victory, but not victory in any real sense."[41]

By rejecting von Clausewitz's *objective* elements of victory, it must be admitted that there are no objective elements except one: the opponent's decision to surrender or to flee from the battlefield.

If we disregard those rare occasions when both sides mutually agree on the outcome of the war, most wars have been terminated in an unclear situation in which each side claimed victory. The disagreement about who is the winner and who is the loser is sometimes so fierce as to be a conflict in its own right and a good pretext for a new war.

In the Suez War of 1956, there were four countries involved. Two of them, Britain and France, admitted that they had not won, by forcing their prime minister, in one case, and the government, in the other, to resign. The two other countries, Israel and Egypt, although they had belonged to opposite sides, both claimed victory. The same happened in the Korean War, in the India-Pakistan War of 1965 and in the clash between the United States and the Soviet Union over the missiles in Cuba.

There may even be difficulties in deciding who has won a particular battle. Thucydides tells of a battle between the Corcyraeans and the Corinthians in which both sides put on trophies and proclaimed themselves victors.[42] In modern battles this is very often the case. In May, 1967, a few weeks before the outbreak of the Israeli-Arab War of June, there was a big air battle over the Sea of Galilee. After the battle was over, both the Israeli and the Syrians claimed victory. The Israelis claimed victory because they had shot down six Russian MIGs; and the Syrians claimed victory because they had shot down four French-made Mirages and killed sixty people.

It can be argued that in this case the claims are not comparable since the Israelis had really shot down the planes, and the Syrians just said they had.

This argument can be refuted on the following grounds: (1) There is no way of checking military claims, because anyone trying to check such facts during or immediately after a battle might be arrested as a spy; (2) even if the facts can be checked it is of no use since lies are part of warfare. To claim that four or six planes were shot down is as good as, and sometimes better than, actually shooting them down.

Fabricated news has played an important role in war since ancient times and has sometimes been crucial in determining the outcome of real victories and defeats.

"'Well then,' said Socrates, 'supposing that a general sees that his force is downhearted, and issues a false statement that help is approaching, and by this falsehood restores the morale of his men: on which side shall we put this deceit?' 'I think under Right.'"[43]

Onasander too makes it a maxim to announce favorable news in the midst of battles, even if false.[44] The Byzantine Emperor Leo used to invent and publish accounts of imaginary victories in another corner of the theater of war in order to raise the spirit of his troops.[45] So ancient and so widespread is this custom that it is impossible to tell in times of war a true story from a false one.

To sum up, we may say that theory and practice both lead us to the same conclusion: there can be no victory if there is no defeat. Victory depends on defeat; defeat does not depend on victory. In other words: *if you can do it yourself* (without the consent or help of your opponent), it is defeat; *if you cannot do it yourself* (that is, you need the defeat or the surrender of your opponent), it is victory.

With the help of this definition it is possible to tell defeat from victory not only in small battles but also in full-scale wars. Let us put it to the test by applying it to the Suez War of 1956. What were the results of the war? The British prime minister was forced into retirement. Was it done by the British themselves? As far as we can rely on the British and international press, it was an independent act. No Egyptian, Israeli or American pressure or consent was involved in the decision. The same can be said about the resignation of the French government. It was an independent decision by the French public, press and parliament. On the basis of our definition, Britain and France suffered a defeat.

The Israeli army retreated from the Sinai Peninsula. Was it a dependent or an independent act?

The retreat from Sinai was—as far as Egypt was concerned—an independent act. (It can be argued that the retreat was forced on Israel by President Eisenhower. As the United States was not a participant in the war, the retreat was an independent act as far as the enemy was concerned.) If it was an independent act, then the Israeli claim that it was a victory cannot be supported. It was a defeat.

The Egyptians, on the other hand, regained their sovereignty over the Suez Canal and got back the Sinai Peninsula. Was this achieved independently by the Egyptians? If the British and the French had not evacuated the Suez Canal and if the Israelis had not retreated from Sinai, Egypt would have got nothing. It was completely dependent on actions carried out by Britain, France and Israel. The Egyptian claim that they had won is, therefore, justified.

Another example is that of Arafat. As one who learned the lesson of the former president of Egypt, he also decided to surrender. Why do I say that he decided to surrender? I use the same yardstick that I've introduced before: the decision to recognize the State of Israel in 1988, was an independent one. Nobody forced Arafat to take such a decision. He took it in spite of many of his own supporters who objected. An independent decision such as this, is an official admittance of defeat. The PLO surrendered to Israel after forty years of struggle. Arafat came to the conclusion that he could not beat the Israel Army by conventional means and therefore recognized the right of Israel to exist. We can consider this a complete débâcle.

If the decision of Arafat is a defeat for the PLO, it must mean that it was a victory for Israel. Why? Because Israel didn't achieve this result due to its own efforts. It only achieved it because the PLO admitted defeat. This case is so clear-cut that we can put the White Flag Principle to the test. As everyone knows, a scientific theory is tested not by its ability to explain the past but by its ability to predict the future. And our prediction for the future is: since the PLO has admitted defeat, it will be rewarded by obtaining a Palestinian state. Israel will be punished for its victory by having to give back all the territory that it conquered in 1967 to the newly established Palestinian state. This prediction almost came true at Camp David, but at the last moment, just as the Palestinian nation was going to be established, the Palestinians changed their mind and started a new war, called the Al-Aqsa Intifada. They did it at first by stone-throwing and later by suicide bombing, and so they lost their independent state. However, this war has not yet ended and so it is too early to predict the outcome.

This "do-it-yourself" yardstick takes the result of war—achieved by blood and misery—out of the hands of speculators and makes it easy for everyone to participate. However, our job of clearing up the mess surrounding the definition of defeat and victory by von Clausewitz and other military theoreticians will not be complete unless we relate the results of war to the question: What are the best and the worst outcomes of war?

When Captain Liddell Hart stated that the object in war should be a better state of peace (see page 6), he meant a better state of peace after the war than before. If we have a state of peace and are not happy with it, we just have to find out what is wrong and then wage a war in such a way that the postwar situation will be better than the prewar situation.

How can we determine and compare two states of peace? Enough statistical data are available today in any given time to determine the state of a country in comparison with other countries or in comparison with the same country at a different time.

If such a comparison is made, two things will be clear. First, it will be apparent that such a thing as a better postwar situation can never have a general or absolute meaning. Results of war, whether defeat or victory, never bear the same fate for everybody. What is gain for one is loss for the other and vice versa. Some profit by victory, others by defeat; some lose by victory, others by defeat. The habit of talking about a country as *one unit* in respect to the outcome of war is nonsense. Instead of talking about *the country's* being worse or better off after a war, it is more nearly correct to speak of *who* in the country is worse or better off after a war. "A lost war," says Max Weber, "as well as a successful war, brings increased business to the banks and industries."[46] A lot has been written on the devastation of the country and the cities in Russia during Napoleon's march on Moscow and his retreat (1812). French soldiers starved to death. An eyewitness of Napoleon's retreat, Baron Boris Uxküll, entered Vilna just after the French army had left it. He found that the city was in full trade boom. "And, in general," wrote Uxküll in his diary, "business doesn't seem to have suffered from the headlong retreat of the enemy, for the shops are well supplied, and for money you can get anything you like."[47]

After the First World War some kings were dethroned. In this sense one may be right in stating that defeats may be bad for kings. Business, however, has never suffered from defeat. More people have been enriched out of the black market than out of the New York Stock Exchange. Though it is true that poor people tend to get poorer after a defeat, it is also true that they tend to get poorer after a victory. Poor people tend to get poorer in any situation. The middle class, on the other hand, may suffer immediately after a defeat, but they are the first to recover and it does not take them long to be better off than anybody else.

In 1815, under the Second Treaty of Paris, which marked the final collapse of the Napoleonic empire, France was required to pay 750 million francs to her victorious enemies in three years. A further condition required her to meet individual claims of people who had suffered at the hands of the French army during its "formidable" victories. All in all, adding also the fixed interest, the amount that France had to pay amounted to over 1,050 million francs. If defeats were really disastrous to their countries, France would not have been able to pay this sum without going bankrupt. "Alas," said men of property as they watched the fatal tumbrel going to be loaded up in the Rue Vivienne, "alas, there goes our money on its way out of the country; next year, we shall go down on our knees before a crown piece; we shall be ruined and reduced to beggary; all enterprises will fail; borrowing will be impossible; and we shall be faced with decline, stagnation and civil death."[48]

But this did not happen. On the contrary, France's economy boomed as it never had before: "To the amazement of all students of finance, the payments were made with ease, credit improved, loans were oversubscribed, and during the whole period of this superpurgation the rate of exchange, that infallible index of the circulation of money, remained in our favour; in other words, there was mathematical proof that more money was coming into France than was going out of it."[49] (Compare the prosperity of the French after their defeat by Germany in 1815 with the collapse of the Wall Street stock market after the American victory over the Taliban in 2002.)

The second thing that will be clear if such a survey is carried out is that the *best* and *worst* outcome of war are meaningful only if they are related to one's own prewar situation and not to that of the enemy. *Victory* and *defeat* are terms describing the position of belligerents vis-à-vis each other at the same time; the *best* and *worst* outcome of war are terms that describe the position of the same country at different times. The two sets of terms (*victory* and *defeat*, *best* and *worst*) have no correlation whatsoever between them. If the aim of war is to improve one's prewar situation, then the war should be conducted not toward victory (compelling the enemy to submit to one's will) but in such a way that the state of peace after the war will be better than the state of peace before.

A few examples will illustrate this point.

We have a state of peace with too much unemployment. We

launch a war and keep it going until enough damage is done to guarantee full employment for years to come. "An army," wrote Lewis Mumford, "is a body of pure consumers. . . . It tends to reduce towards zero the gap in time between profitable production and profitable replacement . . . and nothing ensures replacement like organized destruction."[50]

We have a state of peace with too many debts—national, foreign and private. The more we pay our debts, the more we are in debt since debts can be paid only by debts. If we launch a war and are defeated, we don't have to pay our debts, especially when we add a revolution to defeat. It is a matter of principle for revolutionary governments not to pay the debts of their reactionary forerunners.

We have a state of peace with an old-fashioned and out-dated industry. The factories are old, the machinery is rusty, the management is inefficient and labor relations are corrupt. Exports are failing because competitors are working on much more modern lines. There is no way to improve matters except by demolishing the whole system and rebuilding it from scratch. We cannot do it. No sane society can demolish its own industry even for a good reason. Only an enemy can do it.

We had social troubles in our peaceful prewar situation. Friction among various groups endangered the existence of the whole community. What is needed to unite the people is a major catastrophe. This can be achieved only by war, especially an unsuccessful one.

The more we search for examples to illustrate this point, the more examples we find. It is evident that there is no weakness or fault in a nation, a country or a society that a good defeat cannot cure. Until now there was one solution—victory. But victory as a medicine has been found to be worse than the disease. Now, with our new definitions, defeat is within everyone's reach since *you can do it yourself*.

However simple and easy, a military disaster cannot be achieved in one go. There are some necessary preparations as well as other prerequisites. The progress toward the final disaster must be made carefully in stages, the first of which is *the establishment of a bad foreign policy*.

THREE

Managing a Bad Foreign Policy

ANY ATTEMPT TO EXPLAIN WHAT a bad foreign policy is must start with what it is not. A bad foreign policy is not the misadministration or corruption of good policy, nor is it a passive policy of doing nothing while waiting for things to happen. A bad foreign policy is an active policy, internally consistent, with its own means and ends.

Since the aim of a bad foreign policy is one's own defeat and the enemy's victory, the first objective of such a policy is to have an enemy. The second is to get rid of allies. Allies tend to come to the rescue in critical moments and thus make defeat difficult.

To make an enemy, we must know what kinds of enemy there are. As far as military disasters are concerned, there are two kinds of enemy, *contiguous* and *noncontiguous*. A contiguous enemy is one that is a neighbor and shares a border. He must also have sufficient self-confidence to accept our challenge. The enemy's self confidence is essential because a lack of confidence will keep him from being our enemy, however strenuous our efforts.

It is hardly necessary to point out that a contiguous enemy is always preferable to a noncontiguous one. But circumstances may make it impossible for an enemy to be contiguous, as in the case of an island country. For island countries like Great Britain, Cyprus, Malagasy, Australia, New Zealand or Japan, a contiguous enemy is out of the question. Having only noncontiguous enemies creates problems that are not easy to overcome.

In a letter to Bormann, Adolf Hitler wrote: "A glance at history, both ancient and modern, will show that overseas enterprises have always in the long run impoverished those who undertook them. They have all, in the end, been exhausted by their efforts; and, in the inevitable nature of things, they have all succumbed to forces to which either they themselves have given birth or which they have themselves reawakened. What better example of this than the Greeks?"[51]

If we need the enemy only to present him with our surrender, then any enemy will do. But if the enemy is needed for the purpose of invading our country, then we must make sure that he is capable of doing so. This depends on his technical capacity or on his industrial and economic potential.

Countries with lesser means at any one time but with an untapped economic potential have proved that in situations of great emergency they are capable of materializing this potential. The United States, for example, entered two world wars with inadequate means, but it caught up rapidly because of its enormous economic and industrial potential.[52] The moral of this provides us with our main maxim for choosing a noncontiguous enemy: *Never make a noncontiguous enemy that lacks adequate technical means or economic potential.*

That such a warning is not superfluous can be seen from the example of the Vietnam War.

The United States and Vietnam were (and are) noncontiguous; therefore they were not ideal opponents for our purposes. This was a good war for North Vietnam and the Vietcong because the United States was an excellent enemy. The North Vietnamese could have surrendered at any time and their surrender could have easily been followed by an American invasion. (The Vietcong were spared this because their country had already been invaded.) For the United States, however, the Vietcong and the North Vietnamese were poor enemies. If the United States army had been defeated, there was not the slightest chance of a Vietnamese invasion of the United States.

However, our maxim does not hold for a contiguous enemy, because a common border is easy to cross. The economic-industrial backwardness of a contiguous enemy is no obstacle to invasion. On the contrary, the backwardness of a contiguous enemy can be regarded as an added advantage: the more backward and the more primitive the enemy, the more eager he is to conquer and invade someone else's territory.[53]

There are two ways of making enemies. A contiguous enemy is made by a *territorial claim*. A noncontiguous enemy is made through an alliance with the *enemy's contiguous enemy*.

If a country has a common border with us, we have to dispute this border. To dispute a border means that we have a territorial claim over a part of our neighbor's territory. When we make a territorial claim, our neighbor immediately becomes our enemy. This is universally true, regardless of our former relations with the same neighbor. The friendliest neighbor will become our fiercest enemy the moment we claim a part of his territory.[54]

Three different kinds of claims are possible to someone else's territory: a *legal claim*, an *emotional claim* and an *accidental claim*.

A legal claim is a claim based on legal documents.[55] If the countries involved have been neighbors for a long time, there will be no lack of legal documents to show that at one time or another, parts of the neighbor's territory lay within one's own borders. The longer the countries have been neighbors, the more documents of this type will exist.[56]

The quantity of documents to back the territorial claim is important. The more documents there are, the fiercer the enemy and the more determined he is to resist the claim. Although the number of documents is important, the size of the territory claimed is not. Experience has confirmed that people tend to attack and defend small territorial claims with the same viciousness that they defend or attack large ones.

Just as the size of the territory claimed is unimportant, so too is the strategic or economic value of it. Two examples will illustrate this point. On 9 April 1965, a fight broke out on the Rann of Kutch, the frontier between the Indian state of Gujarat and West Pakistan. The Rann (desert) of Kutch, which covers an area of about 8,400 square miles, has been described as "a vast expanse of naked tidal mudflats, a black desolation flaked with saline efflorescences . . . it is uninhabited and economically valueless." This did not prevent the Indians from claiming it on the ground that "the whole of the Rann formerly belonged to Kutch, and hence was part of India when the state acceded to the Indian Union in 1947." In support of this claim the Indians cited maps and other official doc-

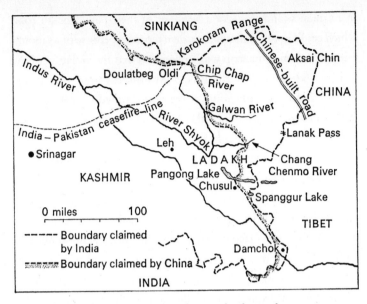

The area in dispute, with the Chinese-built road.

uments issued between 1871 and 1947, when Sind was under British rule. Pakistan claimed the same territory on the grounds that about 3,500 square miles of the Rann lying north of the 24th parallel were formerly under the control and administration of Sind. It also contended that the Rann is a landlocked sea or boundary lake, and under international law the boundary must run through the middle of the area. This argument was rejected by India, on the ground that the British Government of India decided in 1906 that it was more nearly correct to define the Rann as a marsh than a lake.[57]

The second example is the clash between India and China in 1965. It was caused by claims to a tiny strip of land on a deserted mountain, inhabited by no one. The Chinese used this small strip of no-man's-land to carry a segment of their new Tibetan road which could not be built on their own territory because of its mountainous terrain. This strip was so deserted that the violation of the border was spotted by the Indian government long after it had occurred. Rumors circulating at the time credited the discovery of the Chinese road on Indian soil to U.S. army intelligence, who spotted it in photographs made by U-2 spy planes. That this piece of land was unimportant and unnecessary for the Indians did not prevent their government from claiming it. The Chinese immediately brought forward a document to show that before the present international border between India and Tibet, the land belonged to Tibet, which was—according to another document—a part of China. As a self-respecting government, India tried to regain this strip of land by force. The outcome of the war is not so important as the fact that, from that time, the former ally was an enemy.[58]

The legal claim is the best of all territorial claims, but sometimes—when contiguous countries have a short common history—legal documents cannot be procured. In this case the emotional claim should be used.

Emotional claims are inferior to legal claims because they do not irritate the enemy as much as legal ones; nevertheless, they have their own merits. Emotional claims serve as social and national unifiers. By uniting the people behind the claim as well as behind the rejection of the claim (by the opponent), they make the enmity fiercer.[59] It is much easier—as history has already confirmed—to unite a nation behind an emotional claim than behind a legal claim.

Take the Israeli claim to the Old City of Jerusalem, for example. Before the war of June 1967, few people in Israel suffered from their inability to visit the Wailing Wall or the other Jewish historical sites in East Jerusalem. That free access to Jewish holy places—

part of the cease-fire agreement of 1949 between the Israeli and the Trans-Jordanian (later Jordanian) governments—was never respected, did not bother the Israelis much. This can be shown by pointing out that it never was used as a pretext for retaliation. This situation changed the moment Israel conquered the Old City of Jerusalem. To secure it for any future negotiations, an emotional claim was employed. The Wailing Wall became an emotional pilgrimage spot. Not only religious but even secular Israelis looked upon the wall with tears in their eyes. To give back the Wailing Wall now seems impossible, although its inaccessibility before the war did not cause anyone excessive worry. Thus an emotional claim has generated in people a necessity that was not present in them before, and has united them behind this necessity.

The more one people become attached emotionally to something, the more their opponents become attached to the same thing. The harder the Israelis hold on to Jerusalem, the more the Arabs claim it back.

The third way to dispute a border is by an *accidental claim*. An accidental claim is not accidental, nor is it a claim. In an innocent official publication—a school textbook or a postage stamp, for example—a map of the country is produced. By a "mysterious" printer's error, the map includes within one's own border some parts of the neighbor's territory. This method is very elegant. The elegance of it is that no matter how many explanations are given or how many apologies, the neighbor remains an irritated, vengeful enemy for ever.

The violent border clashes between the Soviet Union and the Chinese on the Ussuri River on 31 March 1969 had been planned beforehand by the Chinese in their efforts to make their allies, the Soviet Union, contiguous enemies. Among the various methods used by the Chinese was an accidental claim, although in this particular case everything was done not to make it look accidental.

In 1964, while a joint committee of Soviet and Chinese diplomats was trying to settle the border dispute between the two governments, a textbook was published in Peking. The textbook, *The Short History of Modern China*, had within it a map of China that included the following territories and countries: Korea, Indochina, Burma, large tracts of land in the regions of the Amur and some territories north to the rivers Ily and Kokand in Kazakhstan. In the Far East, the map included the Russian towns of Komsomolsk, Khabarovsk and Vladivostok, and also the peninsula of Kamchatka.[60]

The accidental claim was not the only claim employed by the Chinese. On 10 March 1963, almost a year before the publication of *The Short History of Modern China*, the *People's Daily* in Peking put forward a legal claim. It recalled the border conference of 1860, in which large tracts of Chinese territory were incorporated into the Russian empire. It shows that a territorial claim does not have to be made in only one way. One, two or all three types of territorial claim can be used in combination. This, for example, is done by the Arabs in their fight against Israel. They base their claim on Palestine on legal documents and emotions and print all of their maps as if Israel does not exist.

These three methods of making contiguous enemies are the only foolproof methods. Attacking a neighboring country without making it an enemy beforehand is too vulgar to be considered a policy and therefore is not dealt with in this chapter.[61]

Until now we have been dealing with the contiguous enemy, the good enemy that is made hostile by a territorial claim. A noncontiguous enemy is a bad enemy since he cannot be made hostile by a territorial claim. A noncontiguous enemy is made by indirect methods. These methods are complicated and never safe and fool-proof, as is the territorial claim.

Countries that are not contiguous to each other cannot claim territories. What they can do is to make an alliance with a country that shares a border with the potential enemy. This country—being contiguous to the enemy—can make a territorial claim. In other words, a noncontiguous enemy is made through an ally.[62]

The United States and Afghanistan are far away from each other and don't share a border. As a noncontiguous enemy, it was not easy for America to drop bombs on the Taliban. They had to find an ally who shared a border and they found it in Pakistan, a contiguous ally of the Taliban. Despite misgivings about a dictator who abolished a democratically elected government and developed a nuclear bomb, Bush had to ally the United States with a dictator in order to turn the Taliban from a noncontiguous into a contiguous enemy. However, not trusting Pakistan completely, the Americans went further and made allies with other countries on the Afghan border— Turkmenistan, Uzbekistan and Kyrgyzstan, all former Soviet states. They even tried to ally themselves with Iran (a member of the "axis of evil"!), but Iran rejected their approach. It all goes to show how difficult it is to have a war with a noncontiguous enemy.

Island countries cannot have contiguous enemies or allies. Making them an enemy is the most difficult of all. The efforts that the United States of America made in the early 1940s to make Japan an enemy and drag her into war can serve as an example of such difficulties. Roosevelt started the process of making an enemy of Japan by freezing Japanese assets and credits in the United States. Then he placed an embargo on the export of aviation fuel and machine tools to Japan. According to Fuller, "This was a declaration of economic war."[63] Nevertheless, the "declaration of economic war" was not sufficient to drag Japan into open hostilities with the United States. On 5 November 1941 Churchill wrote to Roosevelt:

> The Japanese have as yet taken no final decision, and the Emperor appears to be exercising restraint. When we talked about this at Placentia you spoke of gaining time, and this policy has been brilliantly successful so far. But our joint embargo is steadily forcing the Japanese to decisions for peace or war.[64]

On the 20 November 1941 the Japanese government sent to Washington a proposal for a peaceful settlement. Roosevelt ignored the Japanese proposal and answered with a ten point memorandum that was regarded by the Japanese as an ultimatum. Henry L. Stimson, the secretary of war, admitted before the Congress's Joint Committee on the Pearl Harbor Attack, the reason for this ultimatum: "The question was how we should maneuver them into the position of firing the first shot without allowing too much danger to ourselves."[65]

If our noncontiguous enemy has been made through an alliance, we are confronted not only with an enemy but also with an ally. As long as we depend on the ally to be on bad terms with our enemy, there is always the danger that our ally will improve his relations with our enemy (after all, he has his own interest to look after!) and we might find ourselves facing two allies and no enemy. Having an ally is in itself an obstacle even if this ally does not change sides. As was pointed out above, besides making an enemy, we have also to get rid of allies. If, through making an enemy, we acquire an ally, we must remember that before the time comes to face the enemy we must get rid of that ally. When we are getting rid of the ally we must again be careful not to lose the enemy as well.

Having made our enemy, we must secure him for the forthcoming war. There is no safe way to keep an enemy. However, since nationalism and patriotism are so deeply rooted in present-day society, there is little danger that a territorial claim—once made—will ever be forgotten. But as long as there are chances—however small—that the enemy might change his mind, precautions must be taken. As there are no foolproof ways to secure a given enemy, the best guarantee of not being suddenly deprived of an enemy is to make as many enemies as possible.[66] A situation can be regarded as ideal if one succeeds in turning all one's neighbors into contiguous enemies, as is the case of Israel today.

After making enemies in the way proposed, there is a good chance that the second objective of a bad foreign policy—getting rid of allies—will not have to be carried out, because there will be no allies left. In case some allies still remain, the best way to get rid of them is by expelling their diplomatic delegation.

To get rid of an ally's entire diplomatic delegation, it is sufficient to get rid of one diplomat only. This is done by declaring one of the ally's diplomats a *persona non grata*. Everyone takes it for granted that a foreign diplomat is also a spy for his country.[67] By expelling a diplomat or just by declaring him *persona non grata*, people will assume that he was caught in the act of spying. As long as foreign diplomats have extrajudicial privileges, they cannot be put on trial (this saves us the trouble of proving our allegations). However, the diplomat's expulsion will start a chain reaction. Since no respectable country can allow the expulsion of a diplomat to go unpunished, one of our diplomats will soon be expelled. Our answer must be an expulsion of another diplomat and so on until, at the end of the diplomatic vendetta, nothing remains of the diplomatic delegation in either country. Countries that do not have diplomatic relations cannot be regarded as allies.

As an example of such an operation let us refer to the front page of the London *Times* of 7 May 1969:

POLAND EXPULSION ANGERS DANES

The Danish Government protested today to the Polish Foreign Ministry over the expulsion of Mr. Ole Brahe-Pedersen, Danish agricultural attache, yesterday. This was an unfriendly act that would harm the good relations between Poland and Denmark. A note said the attache, who has been stationed in Poland since 1962, had given no cause for complaint, and his expulsion therefore appeared to be an unjust and arbitrary retaliation for Denmark's recent expulsion of Stanislaw Niciejewski, a diplomat, for spying.

When getting rid of allies one must be careful not to get rid of them by making an alliance with their enemies. Even if it is true that by making an alliance with an ally's enemy one ceases automatically to be an ally, this is not recommended on the following ground.

By making an alliance with the ally's enemy one is getting rid of an ally but gains another—the ally's enemy. The balance of allies in this case does not change. What we have done is merely exchange one ally for another.

There are two other methods of getting rid of allies which are not recommended. One is playing the role of the mediator and the other is the cordial treatment.

The nature of many modern political disputes today is such that few solutions to a national conflict are satisfactory, and most, if not all, of the satisfactory solutions are not acceptable to both parties. This makes mediation in such disputes almost impossible. By playing the role of a mediator between the ally and a third party, there is a good chance of losing the ally without gaining one. But such an outcome is not always the case. Britain lost both the Israelis and Arabs as her allies when she tried to mediate between them before and during the 1948 war. The same can be said of the efforts of the United States to mediate between the Turks and the Greeks in the Cyprus dispute; her efforts caused anti-American demonstrations in Greece and in Turkey. But on the other hand, the friendship between India and the U.S.S.R., and between Pakistan and the U.S.S.R., became stronger after the Russians played the role of mediator at Tashkent in 1965.

A similar warning must be raised against the use of the *cordial treatment*. It cannot be denied that the United States lost the sympathy of the people in Europe and Asia as a result of cordial treatment such as the Marshall Plan and her other political and economic charities. But this is such an expensive way of getting rid of allies that only the United States can afford it.[68] For countries with normal budgets, there is no substitute for the expulsion of the diplomatic delegation as the cheapest way of getting rid of allies.

FOUR

Ruining a Flourishing Economy

THERE ARE MANY WAYS TO RUIN a flourishing economy.[69] The cheapest way, however, the one we strongly recommend, is to do nothing and let the economy ruin itself. Economists have long since discovered that the natural trend of every economy is more toward disaster than toward prosperity. "The principle of gravitation," states Ricardo, "is not more certain than the tendency of such laws to change wealth and power into misery and weakness."[70]

The doomsday prophecies of Malthus, expressed in his law about the geometrical increase of world population against the arithmetical increase of food supply,[71] have not left the human race a prospect any better than poverty and hunger. For Karl Marx, the inevitability of the ultimate collapse of the most prosperous economy, the capitalistic, was the starting point for devising a completely different social and economic system.[72]

This view was not confined to the mercantile or classical economic schools. Keynes, the founder of modern economic philosophy, expressed similar opinions: ". . . yet, the larger our income, the greater, unfortunately, is the margin between our incomes and our consumption. So, failing some novel expedient, there is, as we shall see, no answer to the riddle, except that there must be sufficient unemployment to keep us so poor that our consumption falls short of our income by no more than the equivalent of the physical provision for the future consumption which it pays to produce today."[73]

The reason why every economy must, eventually, ruin itself can be summed up as follows: When an economy is analyzed at any given time, it is found to be either in a state of *inflation* or in a state of *deflation*, also known as *depression*.[74] If it happens that the economy is not in one of these two states, we find a mistake in the interpretation of the events afterward. A good example is the American economic "boom" of 1926-28, which was found afterward to be nothing but the prerequisite for the Great Crash and the disaster of 1929-39.

Not long ago, Germany was believed to be in a similar boom, which is not depression or inflation but an economic "miracle." This "miracle" worried Germany and the world at large no less than depression or inflation. From time to time distant echoes of fear reached the press. On 11 May 1969 the *Observer* published a report from its Bonn correspondent, headed:

BONN WILL TRY TO LOSE MONEY

The West German Government will probably consider on Wednesday the "substitute economic measures" it could take to halt the rush into deutschmarks. . . . The German Chancellor,

Kurt Georg Kiesinger, has canceled his plan for spending the weekend at his retreat in Southern Germany. The Chancellor will chair the meeting of the "Economic Cabinet." . . . The meeting will consider measures to force speculators to withdraw the enormous flood of "hot money" held in Germany and to reduce the country's enormous balance of payments surplus. . . .

Ignoring dubious "miracles," we are left only with inflations and depressions. Inflations, as we all know, are no good because if they are not checked in time they ruin the economy. There is only one known way to stop inflation, and that is deflation. If we succeed in getting rid of inflation, we have depression instead.

It goes without saying that depression is disastrous and if not checked in time it brings the economy to a standstill. The only way to stop depression is by inflation. This, as we have already seen, is a calamity that can be checked by deflation (that is, depression), itself no better. The economy can be saved from one disaster only by another disaster of equal significance. "If the equilibrium is sensitive, there is a considerable danger of fluctuations in prosperity. We then live in an unstable world, in which we are constantly threatened with inflation and deflation."[75]

Since the economy is perpetually ruining itself, might we rightly ask how we happen to have a flourishing economy in the first place?

As we have already pointed out, there is no better sign that everything will shortly go bankrupt than a prosperous economy. If we happen to have such an economy, it can only mean that disaster is around the corner. In this case, all we have to do, if there is something left for us to do, is to give the economy a slight push in the direction it is already heading. That is, if the economy is heading toward depression, we should push it toward depression; if it is heading toward inflation, we should push it toward inflation.

How to push an economy one way or another is a technical problem that any trained economist can easily manage. If the economy is heading toward inflation, we push it this way by spending more money on public works, by reducing taxes, by lowering the rate of interest and by announcing that we are going to devalue the national currency. There is no better way of encouraging an inflation panic (which is very helpful in such circumstances) than by an official announcement of a forthcoming devaluation. It goes without saying that our promise to devalue should not be carried out, since it is an anti-inflatory measure.[76]

If the economy is heading in the other direction, in that of depression, we give it a push by halting all public works, by cutting off subsidies to industry, commerce and social services, by increasing the taxes, by raising the rate of interest, and so on. We should not rule out an official announcement to devalue the national currency or, better still, to go back to the gold standard.

In our efforts to ruin a flourishing economy we must be careful not to improve it. Though it happens quite often that by trying to improve a ruined economy we make things worse, this is a method that cannot be relied upon. In the underdeveloped countries of Africa and Asia, for example, all attempts to improve the economy have been successful—that is, they made it worse. On the other hand, when the Conservatives came to power in Britain in 1970 and tried to improve the economy, the situation became so muddled that inflationary and depressionary symptoms, which usually cancel each other out, remained active side by side. On 20 July 1971, the London *Times* reported on its front page that the Chancellor of the Exchequer was so shocked by this strange phenomenon that he had lost all faith in the science of economics.[77]

Before we move on to the next prerequisite for defeat, there is still one point to clarify: the timing of the economic ruin. To make the best of it, the economy must be ruined before the battle with the enemy starts. On the other hand, if the economy is brought to a standstill too far ahead of war, there may still be time for a recovery. As the example of the economic recovery of the United States in 1939-40 clearly shows, an economic recovery before the beginning of hostilities may prevent defeat altogether.

Although this caveat has been proven correct time and time again, we have to be on our guard, because the economy has mysterious laws that no one fully understands. This can be seen from the behavior of the stock exchange not only in New York, but around the world, in the aftermath of the terrorist attacks of 9/11. The first reaction on the morning of the twelfth was a slight decline in the price of the shares. There was no doubt in the mind of the public that America would react militarily, but the economy as a whole was not sure about the outcome of such a war. When the dust settled, the reaction of the market became clear. The Taliban had been completely routed, a great blessing for Afghanistan. The country was liberated and the women got rid of their burkas and returned to schools and universities. At last, democracy had a chance of being established. Even their currency increased in value. However, at the same time, the victorious American economy went into a decline that had not been seen for many years. The stock market collapsed: the price of their shares hit rock bottom and the value of their pensions dwindled. The value of the dollar fell and, at the time of writing, is about equal to the euro. This shows us that while the ruin of the economy can help us be defeated, one of the ways to ruin an economy is a victory in war. Is there a moral somewhere? Are we going to see an American military defeat in the near future? Only time can tell.

FIVE

Disuniting a United Society

OUR FIRST STEP IN DISUNITING A united society is to examine the bonds that hold society together. According to Lewis Coser, "Conflict is seen as a binding element between parties that previously have stood in no relation to each other."[78] This opinion is shared by others, among them Georg Simmel and Ralf Dahrendorf.[79]

If conflict is the unifying element in society, what can tear society apart? Strange as it may seem, conflict is also a destructive force. Conflicts create such friction and tension among people that, in the end, they come to hate each other more than they hate the enemy.

The peculiar nature of conflict has baffled many sociologists. "But does conflict always re-establish unity," wonders Coser, "or does it happen only under a specific set of circumstances? We are led to ask: if conflicts unite, what tears apart?"[80]

The study of social conflict has sustained many academic

careers.[81] The results may be summed up as follows: there are two distinct patterns of conflict distribution. One binds society and the other disunites it. The pattern of conflicts that unite society is that which is distributed randomly and forms a *matrix*. In other words, each conflict is so distributed among the population that the people that are grouped together in one conflict are not grouped together in another. "We might suppose," says Dahrendorf, "that in a country there are three dominant types of social conflict: conflict of the class type, conflict between town and country, and conflict between Protestants and Catholics. It is of course conceivable that these lines of conflict cut across each other in a random fashion, so that, *e.g.*, there are as many Protestants among the ruling groups of the State as there are Catholics and as many town-people in their denomination as there are country-people."[82]

This is the type of conflict pattern that unites society. The more numerous the conflicts and the more random their distribution, the stronger the matrix that unites that society.

If, on the other hand, we have conflicts that are so distributed that the same people in one conflict group are also members in another conflict group, then the pattern is not a matrix but a split. We can imagine a society with the same types of conflicts as in the above example, but distributed in such a way that all the Protestants belong to the ruling class and are all town dwellers. In this case there will be a split between the two groups. One group will consist of Protestant-urban-rulers and the other of Catholic-countrymen-ruled. "A society . . . ," says Edward Alsworth Ross, "which is ridden by a dozen oppositions along lines running in every direction may actually be in less danger of being torn with violence or falling to pieces than one split just along one line."[83]

If we have a united society it means that we have conflicts of the matrix type. In order to disunite our society we have to change the matrix conflicts into split conflicts.[84]

We start this operation by choosing one conflict out of the several we have and making it the dominant conflict. If one conflict is already dominant—like, for example, the Protestant-Catholic conflict in Northern Ireland or the Anglo-French conflict in Canada—we leave it at that. If there is no dominant conflict, we intensify and activate one to make it dominant.

Let us assume that in a given society we have chosen class conflict to be dominant. We intensify and activate it by harsher exploitation of the working classes. We cut down their wages; we lengthen their working hours; we cut off their social benefits, and so on. While exploitation is increased, we seal all the safety valves: we outlaw strikes and demonstrations and restrict freedom of speech. The sealing of the safety valves makes the conflict more acute. People suffer *physically* by having less income and working more hours and *mentally* by frustration. Wildcat strikes and unlawful demonstrations are on the increase. This gives the police and the army an opportunity to handle the unsatisfied masses with brutality. Police and army brutality are excellent for intensifying conflicts. As pointed out by Frantz Fanon, violence contributes to conflicts by establishing unity inside the conflict groups. "The practice of violence binds them together as a whole, since each individual forms a violent link in the great chain, a part of the great organism of violence which has surged upwards."[85] This has been tested on many occasions and has never failed.

To intensify a conflict, it is also necessary for the participants to be idealistic. "Conflicts in which the participants feel that they are merely the representatives of collectivities and groups, fighting not for self but only for the ideals of the group they represent, are likely to be more radical and merciless than those that are fought for personal reasons. Elimination of the personal element tends to make conflicts sharper, in the sense of modifying elements which personal factors would normally introduce."[86]

If the dominant conflict is not class but religious conflict, the best way to intensify it is by adopting one of the religions as the official state religion and outlawing the others. If, for one or another reason, it is impossible to outlaw a religion, discrimination will also do. In religious and racial conflicts, political assassination is of great help. It is difficult to account for the sharp intensification of the racial conflict in recent years in the United States without reference to the assassinations of the Kennedys, Malcolm X and Martin Luther King. Similarly, the assassination of Tom Mboya in Kenya in 1970 intensified the tribal conflict between the Luo and the Kikuyu.

While the dominant conflict is intensified, we start to rearrange all the other conflicts so that they are superimposed on one another. If, for example, the dominant conflict happens to be class conflict and among the other conflicts in the matrix there is a peasant-landlord conflict, the latter can be superimposed on the former by a process of *combination*. Class and peasant conflict are combined into one. This can be easily done by redefining the terms of the conflict. Instead of having one conflict between the proletariat and the capitalists and a different one between the peasants and the landlords, the new conflict is between the *exploited* and the *exploiters*. In this way the peasants and the proletariat find themselves together in one group and the capitalists and the landlords in the other. This was done successfully by the Communists before and during the revolutions in Russia, China and Cuba.

The students, in the May 1968 revolution in Paris, also tried to incorporate class struggle into their conflict with the establishment. As it happened, this was only partly successful. But even this partial success was enough to shake the foundation of the De Gaulle regime. The failure of the May revolution in its later stages cannot alter the fact that for the purpose of disuniting a united society, the incorporation of one conflict into another is not only desirable but practical.

When "secondary" conflicts cannot be combined or incorporated into the dominant ones, we have to replace them by others that can be.

When Marx formulated the doctrine of class struggle, he realized that a split in society is impossible as long as there exists a conflict between different religions. To overcome this obstacle, he replaced the traditional religious conflicts with a new one. Instead of Protestants fighting Catholics and Catholics fighting everybody and both fighting Jews, he made up (under the slogan "Religion is the opium of the people") a conflict between religion and nonreligion. The new conflict did not eliminate the fighting impulses of religious people but modified them. Everybody could go on fighting, but instead of fighting Jews, Protestants or Catholics, the fight was now against religion in general. This new conflict was easily superimposed on the class struggle.

By intensifying the dominant conflict, by incorporating others into it and by replacing those difficult to superimpose by others, we no longer have a matrix but a split. The moment we have a split, our society is—automatically—disunited. However, it may still happen that our matrix conflicts are so numerous and deeply rooted that they cannot be incorporated, changed or removed. In this case, we have to adopt a completely different method. We have to import a new population.

Importing a new population—immigration in short—solves the problem of making a conflict split in one brilliant stroke. Immigrants, as everybody knows, tend to stick together. They live in the same habitats, speak the same language, worship the same gods and concentrate in a few, isolated professions. A conflict split between them and the indigenous community is total. The conflicts are superimposed on each other from the very beginning. African-Americans in the United States, Chinese in Malaya, Arabs in East Africa, French in Algeria, whites in Rhodesia and South Africa, and Jews in Palestine are all examples of conflict splits created by immigration.

One of the greatest advantages of these conflicts is that they are easily regulated. If we wish the race issue to be the dominant conflict, we introduce immigrants from a different race. If religious conflicts are preferred, immigrants of a different religion are chosen. The number of immigrants, something that is easily controlled, can make the conflict more or less intense. If too many immigrants are allowed to settle down, societies may explode instead of merely splitting. A conflict split can become so intense as to turn into a violent confrontation. Such explosions are even better than a fission, because the two sides are not just disunited but totally inimical. This is what happened in 1948 in Palestine with Jews and Arabs. Social conflict is not only a powerful tool for fracturing a society but can be—if extreme—a defeat in itself. An explosion of a conflict split makes a national war obsolete since it makes society its own enemy. In this case defeat is assured whichever side wins.

"But if the present internal dissension continued," wrote Livy more than two thousand years ago, "then the war between Rome and Carthage would be nothing in savagery compared with the civil war which was bound to come to Syracuse, where within the same walls each side would have its own army, its own weapons, its own leaders."[87]

SIX

Building Up an Army
for Defeat

To BUILD UP AN ARMY for defeat, there is no need to dismantle the traditional victory-army and build up a new one from scratch. Every army, however victorious, has suffered sufficient military disasters to show that it already has within it the necessary elements of defeat. All that is needed to convert a traditional victory-army into a defeat-army is to cultivate these elements and to suppress those which lead to victory.

What are the elements of defeat?

The best way to identify them is to consider the state of a fighting army at the moment of its collapse. The situation of an army on the battlefield before the final breakdown (defeat or surrender) can be summed up as follows:

1. The troops are desperate and in low spirits;

2. The troops are hungry;

3. The troops are exhausted;

4. The troops are diminished in numbers (lack of reserves);

5. Weapons are out of order (or lack ammunition).

Each of these factors, even by itself, can cause an army's down-fall. If we can combine all of them, a complete military disaster is inevitable.

Unfortunately, the conditions for a military disaster do not apply equally to good and bad troops. Good troops can withstand desperation, hunger, exhaustion and lack of commanders for long periods; bad troops succumb more easily.[88]

Recruitment of Bad Troops

To recruit bad troops we must see what the qualities of good troops are and how they troops are recruited. The traditional good soldier is a young adult male who is healthy, physically fit and mentally well-balanced. A bad soldier, therefore, is anyone who is not a young adult male, not healthy or physically fit and mentally unbalanced. This is the kind of soldier we are looking for; now we have to consider how to get him.

One thing is certain. We cannot ask bad soldiers to volunteer, since volunteers tend to be good soldiers. The principle in recruitment must be that the more a man does not want to serve in the army, the more he is needed there. The only way to drag bad soldiers into service is by force; by compulsory service. As a compulsory draft system is already operating in many countries, our task is made easier. We do not have to create a special draft system; we can take the already existing system and adapt it to our requirements.

The system of compulsory drafting is based everywhere on the same principles; it varies in matters of detail from place to place. In the United States, to take a specific example, the draft system consists of three stages.[89] The first is *registration*. When a young man reaches the age of eighteen he is required to report to the local draft board, where he is given a *Selective Service number*. The second stage is *classification*. After the young man has registered, the board considers a classification for him. Only one category of registrant is called to military service; this is the I-A class: "*Every male between the ages of eighteen to thirty-five who is available for military service.*" Every other classification affords various degrees of respite from army service. When a young man has been classified I-A, he is actually *recruited*.

To adapt the U.S. draft system for the recruitment of bad troops, one thing only has to be changed: instead of drafting the I-A class, this class must be excluded and everyone else drafted instead.

By drafting registrants not classified as I-A, the army will consist of bad soldiers only: *conscientious objectors* (class I-A-0, class I-0 and class 1-2) and "those not currently classified for service because of failure to attain applicable physical, mental or moral standards' (class 1-Y). Many of the soldiers in the army will be preoccupied with domestic problems since they will be classified as III-A, which includes the "man who has a child with whom he maintains a bona fide relationship in their house. . . . " Also in this category is the registrant whose induction into the armed forces would result in the extreme hardship of his wife, divorced wife, child, parent, grandparent, brother, sister or a handicapped person. "Other kinds of bad soldier will be the "alien who has not been admitted to the

United States" (class IV-0), or people who are spiritually inclined: "regular or duly ordained ministers of religion" (class IV-D).

Besides people unfit for combat, or uninterested in military life because of other commitments, the army will also consist of soldiers needed elsewhere as civilians—in the administration, in the courts, in industry, or in the health service. Class II-A, for example, includes "men whose employment in industry, whose continued service in public office (federal, state or local) or whose activity in scientific or medical research is necessary to the maintenance of the national health, safety or interest." The same will apply to children (under eighteen years of age), their parents and grandparents if they are over thirty-five years of age and the married or unmarried females not included in class I-A.

Moreover, if we do not exclude class I-C ("men already in the armed services . . ."), we shall cause a perpetual redrafting into the army of people who are already in the army. This will provide us not only with an unlimited source of trained and experienced troops (without particularly enlarging the army) but also with angry and irritated soldiers, furious at being redrafted into the service the very moment they have been drafted into it.

Desperation Treatment

Once drafted, new recruits have to be treated as harshly as possible in order to keep their morale low. They must be humiliated, trodden upon, insulted, discredited, dishonored, demoted, degraded and disgraced until they are not sure who their real enemy is—the one on the other side of the barbed wire or the one who commands them.[90] This treatment should start the moment the soldier passes through the gate of the recruiting center; but it should not stop there. Harsh treatment must continue throughout military life until the final collapse. Humiliation of the newly recruited bad soldiers must be consistent and thorough and never left to individual whims of corporals, sergeants and sergeant majors. Special measures must be taken to ensure that on every point, however trivial, the soldier is unjustly treated, that he is dissatisfied and wretched.[91]

In the first day of service, for example, recruits are issued service clothing. Quite frequently it happens that some of the uniforms do not fit. This is a good way to harass a new recruit. However, there are still many recruits who get well-fitting uniforms. Furthermore, even those who are issued ill-fitting clothes manage to become well dressed by exchanging their ill-fitting clothes for those of other unfortunate comrades.

This is an example of the lack of consistency and thoroughness in the traditional harassment of recruits. As regards service clothing, the system of allocation must be so modified as to minimize the chances that a recruit will receive a well-fitting uniform.[92] At the same time, unauthorized exchanging of ill-fitting service clothing must be strictly forbidden.

This is but one example of how to rationalize the harassment of soldiers in an army aiming at defeat. Similar methods should be devised for the allotment of pay, leave and quarters; for enforcing discipline and respect for those of higher rank, and so forth.

Nourishment of Troops

Malnourishment of troops, that is, keeping them hungry or in a constant state of indigestion, is a problem of both quantity and quality.[93] The former is easily solved, but the latter is difficult. The reason why it is difficult to spoil the soldiers' feed is that military

Dimensions of the INFANTRY TROUSERS for the several Sizes of Men.

SCALE OF FIXED POINTS FOR ALL SIZES.

	Inches.
Width of Waistband	1½
Only one Button in front of Waistband. Open in front, with a Fly and Five Buttons. The Fly to extend from top to within 3½ inches above point of Crutch.	
Length of Slit at bottom of Side-Seam	2½

SCALE OF FIXED LENGTHS FOR THE SEVERAL HEIGHTS OF MEN.

Height of Man.	Length of Side-Seam.	Length of Leg-Seam.
Ft. In.	Inches.	Inches.
5 7	45	32½
5 8	45½	32¾
5 9	46¼	33¼
5 10	47	33¾
5 11	48	34½
6 0	49	35¼

SCALE OF WIDTHS.

This Scale is applicable for all Heights, and the same proportions are to be preserved if a more accurate measurement be received from Regiments.

	Small.	Middling.	Large.
	Inches.	Inches.	Inches.
Round the Waist	32	34	36
Top of Front, from Side-Seam to Side-Seam (when Buttoned) .	13	14	15
Round the Thigh, two inches below the Crutch	23	24	25
Round the Knee	18½	19	19½
Round the bottom of the Leg . .	18½	19	19½

Dimensions of the INFANTRY COAT for the several Sizes of Men.

SCALE OF FIXED POINTS FOR ALL SIZES.	Inches.
Depth of Collar behind . .	$3\frac{1}{2}$
Ditto in front .	$3\frac{1}{4}$
Ditto Cuff	$2\frac{3}{4}$
Length of Collar Loop . .	5
Ditto Top Breast Loop	$5\frac{1}{2}$
Ditto Bottom ditto . .	$2\frac{1}{4}$
Distance of the Hip Buttons from centre to centre	$2\frac{1}{2}$
Width of each Skirt at Bottom	5
Width of each Skirt at Top, for all Sizes under 32 in. Waist	$6\frac{1}{2}$
Ditto, from 32 in. to 34 in. Waist	7
Ditto, for all Sizes above 34 in. Waist	$7\frac{1}{2}$

SCALE OF FIXED LENGTHS FOR THE SEVERAL HEIGHTS OF MEN.				
Height of Man.	Length of Back Seam from Collar to Hip Button.	Length of Skirt from Hip Button.	Length of Front from bottom of Collar.	Length of Sleeve from Back Seam.
Ft. In.	Inches.	Inches.	Inches.	Inches.
5 7	$16\frac{1}{4}$	$14\frac{3}{4}$	$15\frac{3}{4}$	$33\frac{1}{2}$
5 8	$16\frac{1}{2}$	15	16	34
5 9	$16\frac{3}{4}$	$15\frac{1}{4}$	$16\frac{1}{4}$	$34\frac{1}{2}$
5 10	17	$15\frac{1}{2}$	$16\frac{1}{2}$	35
5 11	$17\frac{1}{4}$	$15\frac{3}{4}$	$16\frac{3}{4}$	$35\frac{1}{2}$
6 0	$17\frac{1}{2}$	16	17	36

SCALE OF WIDTHS.

This Scale is applicable to all Heights, but may be departed from in the event of a more accurate measurement being received from Regiments.

	Small.	Middling.	Large.
	Inches.	Inches.	Inches.
Round the Body at the Breast	38	40	42
Round the Waist	32	34	36
Width of Sleeve, two inches below Elbow	$5\frac{1}{2}$	$5\frac{3}{4}$	6
Length of Collar at Top	$14\frac{1}{2}$	15	$15\frac{1}{2}$
Ditto, at Bottom . . .	$17\frac{1}{2}$	18	$18\frac{1}{2}$

"Specifications for uniforms in the British army under the command of Field Marshal the Duke of Wellington. From The Queen's Regulations and Orders for the Army, Adjutant-General's Office, Horse Guards, Whitehall, 1 July 1844, the third edition. Published by Parker, Furnival & Parker, London, Military Library, pp. 153-4.

cooking is usually done by amateurs. Food cooked by amateurs can never be trusted. It can be bad; but it can also be good, not to say excellent.[94] Another difficulty arises from the need to have two different mess halls—one for the rank and file and one for the officers. It is important that, while the men are badly fed, the officers are well cared for. Discrimination of nourishment between men and officers must also be publicly acknowledged, so that no soldier will ever think that his misfortune is shared by all. Injustice has not only to be done; it must be seen to be done.

Many great military disasters have been accompanied not only by malnourishment but by a marked food discrimination too. In the Crimean War of 1856-57, it was reported that the men were poorly fed; "There was difficulty in cooking the salt pork and the men had to take it raw. . . ."[95] At the same time, high-ranking officers like Lord Cardigan were dining aboard their private yachts, where they were served gourmet dishes prepared by French chefs.[96]

At another débâcle, at the siege of Kut-al-Amarah in 1915-16, the daily rations issued to Indian troops were four ounces of barley meal, nine ounces of vegetables and one ounce of ghee. At the same time, the officers held a dinner on 28 February 1916 to celebrate the sixteenth anniversary of the relief of Ladysmith. The menu at the dinner was as follows:

Hors d'oeuvres:	Olives of All Nations
Soup:	Cheval d'artillier
Fish:	Sole Trench Sabot
Entrée:	Cutlets Jaipur Pony Superb
Joint:	Horse Loin Shell Trimmings
	Mule Saddle with Bhoosa Sauce

Sweets:	Windy Lizzie Pudding with Flatulent Fanny Sauce
Savoury:	Whizz Bang with Starling on Toast
Dessert:	Liquorice Root Mahaila Squares
	Coracle Chunks Bomb Shells
Coffee:	S & T Special and Arabian
Wines:	Liquorice, Tigris Water, Date Juice, etc.
Cigars:	Relief Special
Cigarettes:	Kut Favorites[97]

If officers are provided with good food, the commander in chief must be cared for even better. His dishes must not just be good, but magnificent—especially when the army is starving, as happens in retreats or sieges. Napoleon, for example, kept Dunand[98] as his personal cook even during the retreat from Moscow, when his army was hardly able to get its teeth near horseflesh.

Discrimination between nourishment of soldiers and of officers can be found in many camps; but, like the allocation of equipment, it is not consistent. At the same time that the kitchens are making every effort to spoil the soldiers' feed, the headquarters is issuing manuals advocating good cooking, as the illustration on page 68 clearly shows.

To be of any practical use, bad cuisine must become an art or a science in its own right, not just an amateurish pastime. It must have rules and principles so that its badness can be officially guaranteed.[99]

Here it should be pointed out that bad cuisine is not the only answer to the problem of unpalatable food. Good or bad food is not necessarily the result of bad cooking or of bad provisions. Many

INSTRUCTIONS.

COOKERY is the art of preparing and softening food by the action of fire, so as to render it fit for digestion. The ordinary operations of cookery are boiling, roasting, broiling, baking, and frying.

Boiling.—When boiled meat is required to contain the largest amount of nourishing matter, it should be placed in the boiler when the water is boiling fast; this boiling should be kept up for a few minutes, after which cold water should be added, so as to reduce the temperature to about 160°, and this temperature kept up for the necessary time. The reason of placing the meat in the boiling water is that by this process the albumen near the surface of the meat becomes coagulated, and thus converted into a sort of shell or crust, which equally prevents the entrance of the water into the meat and the escape of the juice of the flesh into the water.

If, on the other hand, it is required to make good soup from meat, the meat should be placed in cold water, and this brought *very gradually* to the boiling point. The juices of the flesh are thus drawn out into the water, which by the former process was prevented.

Roasting is applied chiefly to meat, and is the application of dry heat. Both in roasting and broiling the heat must at first be considerable and rapid, in order to coagulate the albumen (just as in boiling), and thus retain the juices in the cooked meat.

Baking acts in the same manner as roasting, but meat thus cooked is less wholesome.

Frying is practically boiling in fat, and is considered the least wholesome of all kinds of cookery.

A facsimile of a page from Instructions to Military Cooks in the Preparation of Dinners at the Instructional Kitchen, Aldershot, 40185/2364, H.M.S.O., London, 1878, p. 1 people detest even the most delicious dishes if they are not accustomed to them. Ethnic, national, habitual, religious, educational and psychological factors play a major role in determining people's taste. The best *cordon bleu* meat dishes will be rejected by Indian troops, who would rather starve than eat meat—beef, in particular.

This is by no means an Indian peculiarity. The same would happen to British troops if offered French-style frogs' legs prepared by the best Parisian chefs. French soldiers would be no less disgusted if served English sausages. To serve Israeli troops with such non-kosher delicacies as *fruits de mer*—crabs, lobsters, prawns, shells and oysters—is to force them into starvation, as is the serving of gefilte fish to Arabs.

Drills, Marches, Ceremonies and Exercises

Our troops are disgraced, humiliated and hungry. At the same time, it is also necessary to exhaust them with drill—marches, ceremonies and exercises. Under the pretext of their having to attain perfection, soldiers should be made to march, run, walk, crawl, jump and dive with or without a heavy load for long periods. They should also be marched on parades as often as possible and made to stand at attention for hours in the burning sun or in the pouring rain. Special attention must be given to retreat marches. Soldiers drilled in the traditional way are well versed in how to advance upon the enemy, but they are very poor at escaping from him.[100] Jomini complains that "retreats are certainly the most difficult operations in war. This remark is so true that the celebrated Prince de Ligne said, in his piquant style, that he could not conceive how an army ever succeeded in retreating."[101]

Every commander and observer of battles has noticed that soldiers are no good at retreating. To quote Jomini again: "When we think of the physical and moral conditions of an army in full retreat after a lost battle, or of the difficulty of preserving order, and of the disasters to which disorder may lead, it is not hard to understand why the most experienced generals have hesitated to attempt such an operation."[102]

The retreat march, neglected by the traditional victory-army, is very important for defeat.[103] Its execution is quite different from the regular advance march, though both can be regarded as *"series of movements by which soldiers are moved from one place to another."*[104] These movements are carried out by means of locomotion that, in the case of the infantry, consists of movements of the legs, controlled by vision. In the advance march, the legs and the head are both facing the same direction—the direction of the enemy. In the retreat march it is different. Here the legs and the head are facing opposite directions: while the eyes watch the enemy, the legs are moving away from him.[105] A clear distinction between the two types of marching is demonstrated in the illustrations on page 71.

To make soldiers good at retreating, they must be drilled in the retreat march instead of the traditional advance march. On page 72 are a few examples of the postures, inclinations and movements to be practiced in the defeat-army.

Retreat drills will exhaust soldiers more rapidly than advance drills because they put a greater strain on the body. At the same time, the troops will learn something really useful. In this way, instead of being the "most trying of all operations in war,"[106] retreats will become the easiest, and generals will no longer hesitate to command them, as has happened in the past.

An advance march (side view)

A retreat march (side view)

Saluting to the front

Fix bayonet (rear view)

Retreat march

Stand at ease

Present arms (second position)   *Present arms (third position)*

Front view (first position)   *Marking time (slow and quick)*

Diminishing One's Own Reserves

Diminishing the size of one's own army makes defeat easier. Even von Clausewitz recognized this as a vital condition for military disaster.[107] In fact, there is no problem in reducing the size of one's army, since armies have a natural tendency to reduce themselves even without war. In 1808, Sweden mobilized an army of 17,000 men to resist a possible attack by the Danes. Before the army had begun any operations and even before it left its barracks, 6,800 of the soldiers (40 percent) perished.[108] The same kind of thing happens in every army, though, for obvious reasons, it is not published or admitted.[109]

The natural process of the army's self-annihilation is sure and stable, but as a result of better hygienic conditions and better medicine, it has nowadays become too slow. It is so slow, indeed, that an army is able to replenish its empty ranks with new recruits. For the purpose of defeat and surrender, we need to get rid of troops more rapidly. This can be achieved by making our soldiers brave. "Courage and wisdom," said Antisthenes, "are admitted to be sometimes injurious both to one's friends and to one's country."[110]

It is commonly assumed that the proper spirit for defeat is cowardice and that bravery is the proper spirit for victory. To some extent this is true. In small, tactical engagements timid soldiers are more easily defeated than brave ones. If war were limited to tactics, cowardice would be the proper spirit for a defeat-army. But as a military débâcle on a strategic or a grand-strategic level is more important than a tactical one, it does not seem that cowardice can be of any use. Even in ancient times courage was disastrous. "The exhibition of desperate courage on the part of the English in the battle of Hastings," says Charles Oman, "had only served to increase the number of the slain. Of all the chiefs of the army, only Ansgar the Staller and Leofric, Abbot of Bourne, are recorded to have escaped. . . . The king and his brothers, the stubborn housecarls, and the whole thegnhood of Southern England had perished on the field. The English loss was never calculated; practically it amounted to the entire army."[111]

Germany, Japan and Italy fought the same enemies in the last world war, but they did it with different spirits. Japanese soldiers were the bravest. They never surrendered until ordered to do so by their emperor. Italian soldiers, on the other hand, were the most timid. A comparison between the respective débâcles of the Japanese, German and Italian armies will show that the braver the soldier, the greater the catastrophe that befell him. Italy's surrender cannot be regarded as grave by any standard. If we compare Italy's débâcle with France's victory in 1945, it is difficult to see any difference. Germany's defeat was far more serious, and Japan's surrender the worst.

One specific case will show this more clearly. When General Yamashita attacked Singapore in 1942, he was able, with only 30,000 brave men, to overcome General Percival's huge but timid army. The result was that 100,000 British, Australian and Indian troops marched into captivity. When the same Japanese general succumbed on 2 September 1945, 100,000 brave Japanese soldiers were dead.

It is impossible to escape the conclusion that cowardice, though useful in certain circumstances, is no match for bravery in achieving a complete disaster. Bravery brings about defeat because brave soldiers make themselves better targets for enemy fire than timid ones.[112] In this way, brave soldiers help to diminish their own reserves. It is only the brave who expose themselves to bullets; or, if no bullets reach them, hurl themselves on the enemy with explosives tied to them, as did the Japanese *kamikazes*. The partnership between courage and death has long been known and glorified in verse and prose.

> . . . what's brave, what's noble,
> Let's do it after the high Roman fashion,
> And make death proud to take us . . .[113]

To make timid soldiers courageous is, therefore, one of the most important duties of an army whose aim is defeat. Various schemes have been devised for the initiation of bravery. Awarding medals, for example, is one of them. It is believed that acts of courage, gallantry and bravery are performed and thus awarded when the army is victorious. The study of military history shows quite the opposite: it is only when the army is in a fix that the individual is given a medal. The Victoria Cross—the highest ranking of all British military medals—is awarded to soldiers who have tried (usually in vain) to save their army from catastrophes. The creation of the Victoria Cross itself was made necessary by the combined British, French and Turkish fiasco in 1856-57, and the complete annihilation of the Light Brigade in the Crimean War.[114]

The history of the Victoria Cross since the Crimean War is, in fact, the history not of British victories but of British defeats. "Just as the Crimea will always be connected in the public mind with the charge of the Light Brigade at Balaklava, so the Zulu war will always be remembered for the disaster at Isandhlwana. . . ."[115] This disaster was rewarded by two VCs, one to Lieutenant Malvill and the other to Lieutenant Coghill. The loss of Delhi in the Indian mutiny in 1857 was celebrated by three VCs (Buckley, Forrest and

Raynor).[116] Of the recent VCs—to add a single example—one was awarded by Queen Elizabeth II to Warrant Officer Keith Payne of the Australian army training team for a blunder in Vietnam. According to the citation, Payne got his medal because "Two companies were attacked by North Vietnamese using machine guns and small arms. As the companies broke under heavy mortar and rocket attack Warrant Officer Payne attempted to encourage his troops. . . ."[117]

This is a typical citation for the Victoria Cross or for any other military medal, decoration or award distributed by any army throughout the world.[118] All illustrate the point that wherever there is a blunder there must be a medal, and whenever there is a medal for bravery there must have been a blunder.

Another way to incite bravery in timid soldiers is by a demonstration of bravery by the commander.

There are two ways to lead soldiers into battle: one is with the commander at the rear and the other with the commander in the lead. When the commander remains in the rear, soldiers are timid. They show courage when the commander leads them in front. By *commander* we do not mean only the commander in chief but also the junior commanders such as the lower rank of officers and even the NCOs—anyone, in fact, who leads troops into battle. "In combat you have to be out in front leading them (the troops), not directing them from the rear. The men say, 'If the officer's going to stay back a hundred yards, then I am going to stay with him.'"[119]

Personal example is also useful in getting rid of the commanders themselves. When commanders lead their troops from behind, they survive their armies even in gigantic catastrophes. Napoleon survived not only the destruction of his army but the destruction of his empire as well. In classical times the same happened to Hannibal. This is also true about General Lee, Chiang Kai-shek, Emperor

Hirohito and many others. When contemplating a military disaster it is very important to allow situations in which those who send others to die save their own skin. The Japanese general Tominaga used to deliver to his *kamikaze* pilots thc following speech:

> When men decide to die like you, they can move the heart of the Emperor. And I can assure you that the death of every one of you will move the Emperor. It will do more—it will even change the history of the world. I know what you feel now as you put the sorrow and joys of life behind you for you will become gods. Soon I hope to have the privilege of joining you in your glorious death.[120]

Did General Tominaga join them in their glorious death? No. At the last moment he fled to Formosa. General Yamashita, the commander of the Japanese forces in the Philippines, tried to court-martial Tominaga for desertion, but with no success.[121]

That such a thing could happen in the Japanese army shows that, after all, the Japanese army was not a perfect instrument for defeat. It can explain their victories in the first phase of the world war. In a perfect defeat, army commanders must always be in the lead and show their subordinates the heroic way of dying for their country.

Weapons Out of Order

While reducing one's own army, great care must be taken not to harm the enemy. This is exactly what the factor—weapons out of order (see page 85)—stands for. When we say that a weapon is out of order, we may mean one of three things: that it misses the target when fired; that it inflicts damage on one's own troops instead of the enemy's; that it is likely to misfire. Which kind of weapon is most likely to become out of order so that we may arm our troops with it?

After careful study it has been found that the weapon most likely to malfunction is an improved weapon. The modern rifle, for exam-

The art of missing the target as a part of a national education program is already on its way, as can be seen from this comic page, published in the United States. (Giant World's Finest Comics No. 188, Oct.–Nov., 1969, *National Periodical Publications, Inc., Sparta, Ill.*) Copyright © *National Periodical Publications, Inc.*

ple, is an *improved* version of the old musket or carbine. It has three complicated devices to make accurate firing: the foresight, the backsight and the wing gauge. To shoot accurately with a modern, improved rifle, it is not enough to manipulate one, two or all three of these gadgets separately. There must be coordination between them. This is a complicated and difficult task, especially when the wind is blowing. No wonder that troops equipped with modern rifles are unable to stand their ground if they are not supported by machine guns, tanks and other weapons. By improving the rifle even more, by adding more gadgets and devices to make shooting accurate, the rifle can be made totally useless.

It might be interesting to mention that this special feature of the modern rifle was foreseen as long ago as the end of the nineteenth century. When the modern rifle went into service in the French army, Alfred Jarry wrote:

> We disapprove of the innocuousness of the military rifle in several respects: its range exceeding the limits of visibility, such a high bullet velocity and small calibre as to inflict no real wound but only an unimpressive puncture, inability to produce smoke, etc... for the fact is widely known that in the Level 86 the repeating mechanism, if anyone is so imprudent as to use it, invariably jams and puts the rifle totally out of service. We presume the inventor perfected this feature in order to render the weapon worthless to the enemy in the event of defeat.[122]

What was true about the sophisticated rifle of the nineteenth century is certainly true about the super-sophisticated weapons of our time. In 2002 it was reported in Britain that "The Ministry of Defence faces the prospect of having to ditch the new version of the soldier's standard rifle, modified at a cost of £92 million, because it is too difficult to maintain in military operations."[123]

A slow aircraft, flying 300 miles per hour, can hardly miss a target. A pilot flying a modern superjet at Mach 2 or 3 cannot see a target at all, and if he does, it is only for a fraction of a second. This is the main reason why mighty armies with the most sophisticated weapons are unable to overcome poor armies with primitive weapons. The Russians could not overcome the Finns in 1939; the French were defeated by the Vietnamese and by the Algerians; and the mighty United States army could not overcome the North Koreans, the Chinese, the Vietcong and the North Vietnamese through many years of war. The bombing of North Vietnam, to take only one example, caused little real damage, since it is impossible to spot such a small target as a wooden bridge from a high-speed, high-altitude superbomber. Moreover, in their efforts to drop the bombs on the enemy the U.S. pilots quite often dropped them on their own comrades. On 2 August 1968 the *Daily Telegraph* reported:

An American Air-Force jet, supporting Air Cavalry troops in the A Shau valley near the Laos border yesterday, mistakenly directed rockets and cannon fire at an American unit, killing eight and wounding 50. On the previous night, 50 rounds of artillery were fired at an American logistical base two miles from Dong Ha, wounding four servicemen and damaging several buildings. A spokesman said that initial investigations had indicated that the shells were 'probably' fired by an American Fifth Infantry Division artillery unit.

These two incidents brought the total accident casualties in a three-day period to 24 dead and 174 wounded. On Friday, stray fire from American river convoys, caught in two separate Vietcong ambushes deep in the Mekong Delta, killed 16 South Vietnamese and wounded 120. It appears almost certain that Allied accidental casualty figures from Thursday to Saturday will exceed those caused by Communist forces.

A random selection of daily newspapers reveals that the examples cited above were not isolated incidents. Similar things are happening all the time and they have become more frequent as aircraft and other weapons are improved.[124] In the war against the Taliban it was reported that:

> American B-52s began carpet-bombing the al-Qaida caves at Tora Bora yesterday, desperately trying to make headway in an increasingly difficult battle against Arab forces loyal to Osama bin Laden.
>
> Mujahadeen commanders on the frontline struggled to control their frustrated, poorly armed and underfed troops. A week's bombing of al-Qaida positions in the White Mountains south of the Jalalabad plains has come at a price.
>
> Three mujahadeen soldiers were killed on Saturday night when their mountain-top gun post was destroyed by American jets, bringing the number who have fallen victim to the bombing to 18, far more than the Arab forces.[125]

Missing targets with aircraft, though remarkable, is nothing compared to blunders with more sophisticated weapons: chemical, bacteriological and nuclear.

On 27 October 1914 the Germans shelled the British force at Neuve-Chapelle with shrapnel containing dianisidine chlorsulphonate. Three months later, in January, 1915, they used xylyl bromide on the Russian front. "Neither action was a success," states Robin Clarke in *We All Fall Down*.[126] In September, 1915, the British used chlorine gas against the Germans at Loos. This too was a failure.[127]

If chemical warfare in the First World War was not successful, how can so many casualties from gas be accounted for? The Russians were reported to have had 275,000 casualties; the French,

190,000; the British, 181,000; the Germans 78,763 and the Americans 70,552.[128]

If the number of gas casualties is correct, how is it that chemical warfare was regarded a failure? A weapon that can cause 795,315 casualties is anything but a failure. The only answer is that the victims of gas attacks were mainly the soldiers of the combatants who made such attacks. This would also explain why chemical weapons were not used in the Second World War, although every army had these weapons at its disposal.

Chemical warfare can be used not only by spraying it from the air as was done in the First World War, but also by injecting it directly into the body. It would not be easy to inject enemy soldiers with poison chemicals. They might, naturally, object to it. However, there is no reason why it should not be injected into one's own soldier's bodies, under the pretext that it will save them from something worse. It may sound like a stupid joke, but it has been done, and quite successfully, in the Gulf War:

> French forces who served in the Gulf War were not given the vaccines and anti-biological warfare measures administered to British and American veterans and are free from the illnesses that beset their allies, the United States Congress has been told.
>
> Evidence to the subcommittee on national security shows the effort made to protect service personnel from biological and chemical weapons most likely damaged their health.
>
> The French were issued protective suits and not given the cocktail of drugs that British and American servicemen took. Only 140 of the 25,000 French Gulf veterans have reported illnesses related to Gulf War service, compared with more than 5,000 of the 52,000 British troops deployed and 137,862 of the 697,000 United States service personnel.

The French made no use of organophosphorous pesticide, now known to be very dangerous to humans, unlike American and British forces.[129]

An army aiming at defeat should equip its soldiers with chemical weapons. Biological weapons, though not used yet in war, would have a similar effect. Nuclear weapons, the most sophisticated of all existing weapons, are the best with which to equip a defeat-army.[130] When the atom bomb was first dropped on an enemy (in Hiroshima and Nagasaki) it caused about 100,000 casualties. The number of American casualties in the United States from their own bomb is at least fifteen times higher. On 18 December 1969 the *Times* of London reported:

> Two leading scientists with the Atomic Energy Commission (AEC) gave a warning today that permissible radiation pollution could, if unabated, cause more than 64,000 deaths a year in the United States. . . . 'The current standards,' Dr. Gofman said in an interview, 'are based on the theory that there is a threshold of radiation below which no harm accrues to man. However, our research shows that there is no threshold dose demonstrable for man, that any radiation exposure, no matter how slight, causes risks. If everyone received the Federal Radiation Council statutory allowable dose from birth, there would be a five per cent increase in the death rate by age 30.'

Five weeks later this statement was confirmed by another report which said that the death of about 400,000 infants under a year old in the United States and 100,000 in Britain were caused by a specific effect of radioactive fallout from nuclear tests that was not allowed for in safety standards.[131]

It is easy to calculate that the number of American casualties in

the United States during the twenty-four years since Hiroshima (if 64,000 deaths occur each year) has totaled 1,536,000 men under thirty years of age, as compared with only 100,000 in Japan (all ages). This shows that nuclear weapons are the best weapons to inflict casualties on one's own people while they are being improved for future use.

It was not only Americans who suffered from dropping nuclear bombs on Japan. The British have also suffered from nuclear weapons, although they have not yet dropped them on anyone. The mere production and testing of its nuclear weapons was enough to inflict damage.

> More than 22,000 British servicemen helped run and witnessed 21 tests in which nuclear bombs were exploded in Australia, Christmas Island and other Pacific islands between 1952 and 1958.
>
> Twenty years after the tests, many of the servicemen began to complain that they were suffering from cancers and illnesses which they believed resulted from being exposed to radiation in the tests. Many of them have since died.[132]

More revelations about self-imposed victims of the nuclear tests in America appeared in the beginning of 2002. A United States government study says that fallout from cold war nuclear tests by the United States, Britain and the Soviet Union has caused the death of an estimated 15,000 Americans.

The study was conducted by the National Cancer Institute and the Centers for Disease Control and Prevention, but its publication has been delayed by the United States government.

It estimates that 80,000 people who lived or were born in the United States in the past fifty years, have contracted or will contract cancer as a result of nuclear tests conducted in Nevada and the Pacific, Soviet tests in Kazakhstan and eastern Russia, as well as nine British tests on the Christmas and Malden islands in the central Pacific in 1957 and in 1958. The impact of French bomb tests in the Pacific and Chinese tests was not included in the study.

Of that number, 15,000 cases are estimated to be fatal. The study reported that everyone living on the American mainland had been exposed to fallout. "The message is we are all downwinders," said Bob Schaeffer of the Alliance for Nuclear Accountability, a coalition of pressure groups. "The release of this report is long overdue. It is now clear that our own nuclear weapons tests have caused thousands of deaths, not just near the Nevada test site but throughout the United States. . . ." Any person living in the contiguous United States since 1951 has been exposed to radioactive fallout, the study found, "and all organs and tissues of the body have received some radiation exposure." The 1997 report indicates that some farm children—those who drank goat's milk in the 1950s in high fallout areas—were as severely exposed as the worst-exposed children after the 1986 Chernobyl accident, "yet the government did nothing to inform the people in these affected areas."[133]

An army with brave, humiliated, desperate, wretched, hungry and exhausted troops armed with improved and sophisticated weapons is sure to suffer a military disaster. Nothing, in fact, apart from exceptionally good luck, can save such an army.

Good luck remains, unfortunately, the only obstacle to making defeat 100 percent foolproof.[134] To overcome good luck, proper disaster strategies and tactics must be used (see next chapter). If, after all, one still remains lucky . . . well, this is a calculated risk one has to take as long as war remains the only solution to certain national and social conflicts.

SEVEN

Strategy and Tactics

THERE ARE TWO KINDS OF MILITARY disaster: defeat and surrender. They are distinct but dependent on each other. An army can surrender after a defeat, but it cannot be defeated after a surrender. A defeat, however disastrous, can always be followed by more defeats, while a surrender can never be followed by another surrender. Two different sets of strategies and tactics are therefore required: one for defeat and another for surrender.

Strategy and Tactics of Defeat

From a purely strategic viewpoint, defeat is signified by flight from the battlefield. The strategy of defeat is the strategy of flight from the battlefield. The first thing, therefore, that must be considered in such a strategy is the desired severity of the defeat.

How Can Severity of Defeat Be Measured?

Severity of defeat is proportional to the speed and duration of flight; the greater the defeat, the speedier and the longer the duration of the flight of the vanquished. If we denote speed by V and duration of flight by T, the severity of defeat, D, can be expressed by the equation $D = VT$. Since speed multiplied by time equals distance (S) covered, the equation can be simplified to $D = S$.

While speed and duration are variables, the direction of the flight is constant. The vanquished's natural path of flight is along the line of communication,[135] in the opposite direction of their previous advance.

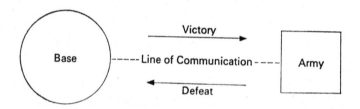

If the army flees along the lines of communication and the severity of the defeat is measured by the distance covered, the line of communication must be sufficiently long if the army is aiming at a disastrous defeat. Because of the length of the line of communication, the defeat of Napoleon in Russia in 1812 was far more severe than the sum of all the defeats of Prussia, Austria and Russia between 1789 and 1812. The same rule holds everywhere. "In both North Africa and Stalingrad—in fact in the whole of Russia," wrote General Fuller, "one common denominator is to be discovered. It is over-extension of German communications coupled with the difficulty of protecting them. From Egypt, Rommel's ran westwards

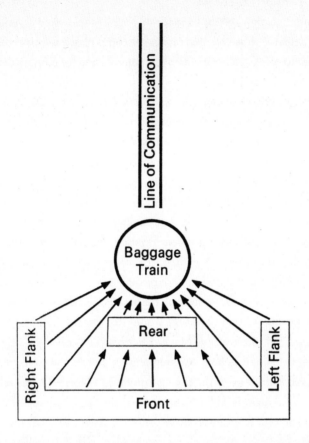

for one thousand two hundred miles to Tripoli, and thence, as the crow flies, one thousand three hundred miles to the industrial centers in Germany—his source of supply. From Stalingrad, Hoth's ran westwards through Russia for one thousand miles, and thence six hundred miles to central Germany."[136] In each case, the severity of the defeat was in direct proportion to the length of the lines of communication.

The first maxim, therefore, for a defeat strategy is that the line of communication should be made as long as the desired severity of the defeat.[137] It is here that tactical victories play a positive role: in order to overstretch the lines of communication for a future defeat, *battles must be won.*

The length of communication lines makes the defeat slight, severe or disastrous; but it does not initially cause it. Defeat itself can only be achieved on the battlefield in a direct confrontation with the enemy. When the army is in a direct confrontation with the enemy, every soldier faces the foe while his back is toward the line of communication. Though good for advance in case of victory, this is a bad position for defeat. In order to flee from the battlefield, the troops must assume a different position: their flank must be presented to the enemy while their front faces the line of communication. Only in such a position is it possible to flee from the battlefield. This, however, does not solve all the problems of defeat. It must also be remembered that, when the troops flee toward the line of communication, their way is blocked by their own rear: the baggage train, the supply depots, the ammunition dumps and so forth.

Even if the way of the fleeing army is not blocked by its rear, a successful flight is still difficult because the line of communication is too narrow to allow an entire army to pass at once. The fugitives must also reach the line of communication with the utmost speed. These problems can be overcome if the army: (a) is broken into small units; (b) is scattered in all directions (so that each unit can reach the line of communication from a different angle, in a different place and at a different time); and (c) gains momentum on its way, so that it reaches the line of communication as fast as possible.

Before proposing the best ways to meet these conditions it should be noted that a guerilla army differs from a regular army in that it is composed of small units and has no baggage train or specific lines

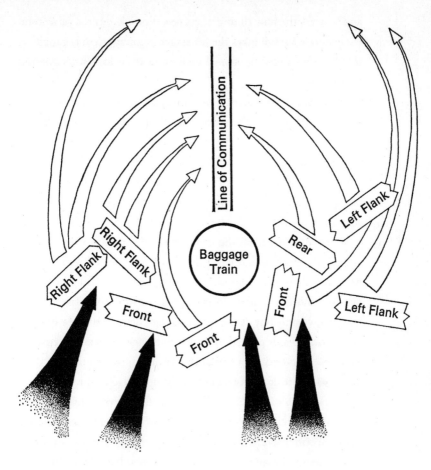

of communication (since the whole country is its base, every path its line of communication). This is why a guerilla army has no difficulty in taking to its heels each time it confronts a regular army.[138]

Unlike the guerilla, a regular army must meet conditions (a), (b) and (c) before it can be successfully routed. To achieve this, the army must engage in battle. When fighting breaks out, the enemy's assault disperses one's own troops into small units (condition a) and scatters them in all directions (condition b). At the same time, the enemy's pursuit gives the necessary momentum to the fugitives for them to reach the line of communication as fast as possible (condition c).[139]

The conditions of defeat (a, b and c) can be satisfied through the enemy's assault. As there are only three ways of assaulting an army—frontal, flank and rear assaults—the number of ways in which an army can be defeated is also limited. In the case of a frontal assault, there are two stratagems by which an army can be put to flight; in the case of flank and rear assaults, there is only one stratagem for each.

When attacked from the front, there is one thing that an army aiming at defeat should never do, and that is defend itself. This is because defensive warfare is the most powerful of all methods of warfare; more powerful, in fact, than the offensive. Trench warfare, to give only one example, is a kind of defensive warfare. In the First World War it proved to be much stronger than all the enemy's assaults. Hundreds of thousands of soldiers were killed in futile attempts to break through entrenched defensive positions.

"In order to express ourselves distinctly," says von Clausewitz, "we must say that the defensive form of war is in itself stronger than the offensive. . . ."[140] As Colonel T. Layman succinctly expressed it: "Put a man in a hole, and a good battery on a hill, and he will beat off three times his number, even if he is not a very good soldier."[141]

If defensive warfare is stronger than the offensive, it is obvious that it cannot be employed for the purpose of defeat. On the other hand, the use of offensive warfare is also out of the question, since it might give the enemy an opportunity to surrender. It looks as if there is no way of being defeated. Fortunately, this is not so. The answer was given by Napoleon himself: "The whole art of war consists in a well-reasoned and circumspect defensive, followed by rapid and audacious attack."[142] In other words, the commander must combine a defensive strategy with offensive tactics. To make the enemy's assault successful, one has to weaken one's own defenses by opening gaps in one's own front line. When soldiers are dispatched to attack the enemy's position, they leave gaps in their own defense. These gaps enable the enemy to break through.

To make perfectly clear how it is possible to be defeated by a combination of defensive strategy and offensive tactics, one famous battle will be analyzed in full. This is the battle of Arbela, in 331 B.C., where the Persian army, under the command of Darius III, was defeated in a pitched battle by Alexander the Great.[143]

The battle of Arbela is usually divided into three phases, each phase distinguished by the formation of a tactical gap of the kind previously described.[144]

Phase One

The battle started with Alexander moving his right flank in echelon to attack the Persian left wing. This was an opportunity for Darius to open a gap in his front by making two offensive moves: (l) the chariots and the cavalry of the Persian left wing were sent to attack Alexander's advancing echelon; (2) the chariots of the Persian center (left of the elephants) were ordered to charge the Macedonian phalanx opposite them.

The dispatch of the cavalry and the chariots from the left wing opened a wide gap in the Persian front which lured Alexander in. He dashed through the gap, threatening the king's rear. Darius seized the opportunity and fled from the battlefield. This action

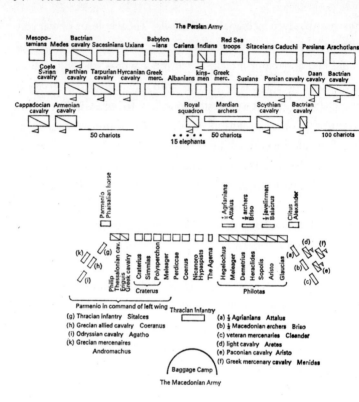

THE BATTLE ORDER AT ARBELA

The positions of the two armies before the battle as reconstructed by Major General Fuller. The Persians were stretched in one continuous front (more extended than shown). The Macedonians, being far inferior in number, covered both wings with flanks composed of infantry and cavalry troops

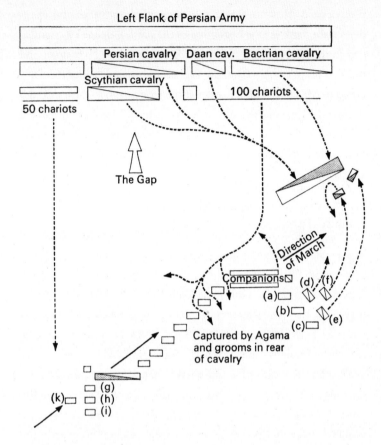

could have sealed the fate of the Persians had their army not been so large. As it was, Darius' flight was not enough to secure the collapse of the entire Persian army.

Phase Two

Once the Macedonian phalanx had beaten off the charge of the Persian chariots, it followed Alexander into the gap which had thus been opened. This movement, together with the advance of Alexander's right flank (at the beginning of the battle), opened a counter-gap in the Macedonian front. Seeing this gap, the Hyrcanian and the Tarpurian cavalry from the Persian right wing (under the command of Mazaeus) could not resist the temptation to dash through it toward Alexander's camp. At the same time, Mazaeus outflanked the Macedonians' left wing. This was a critical moment for the Persian defeat. It looked as if they were going to win despite their king's flight.

Phase Three

The Persian Hyrcanian and Tarpurian cavalry grasped the situation and in a brilliant maneuver, almost unprecedented in history, retreated through the same gap by which they had come in. On the way back they were met by Alexander in person, who had just returned from the pursuit of the king, and were beaten off: This sealed the Persians' fate and their whole army fled in panic.

Though the means of warfare have changed tremendously since the time of Alexander the Great, the principles of defeat remain the same.[145] During the Second World War there were many instances in which huge and powerful armies were defeated in exactly the same manner. When the German army retreated before the Russians, in October, 1943, it halted at the junction of Zhitomir and Korosten. The Russian general Vatutin tried to rout them but without success. To end the stalemate, Field Marshal von Manstein decided to counterattack. This attack opened gaps in the German defenses so that the Russians could break through and continue their advance. Liddell Hart analyzed the situation in a similar way:

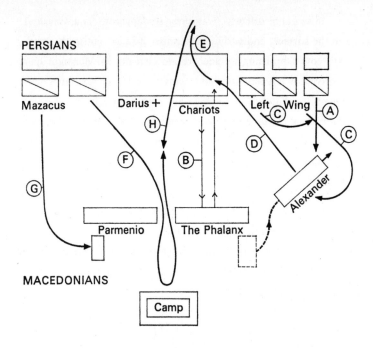

Arbela—situation at the moment of contact

Subsequent main attacks shown thus: → and lettered in order:

A—abortive cavalry attack
B—chariot attack
C—enveloping cavalry attack
D—Alexander's attack
E—Alexander's pursuit
F—attack on Macedonian camp
G—attack on Parmenio's wing
H—return of Alexander

. . . this counteroffensive was never so dangerous as it appeared on the surface, and early in December it faded out in the mud. Moreover, by using up such reinforcements as Manstein had received, it left him without means to meet the Russian's next move. . . . Vatutin, in combination with Koniev from the other flank, now cut off this Korosten salient by a pincer stroke, and surrounded ten enemy divisions. . . . This coup created a gap in the German front, thus easing the way for a fresh Russian progress."[146]

A year later, at the end of 1944, when the Allies' march on the Rhine came to a halt because the German army adopted a defensive attitude, it was only the counteroffensive of Field Marshal Model in the Ardennes which opened a gap through which the Allies could resume their advance.

"This counteroffensive," writes Liddell Hart, "had been a fatal operation. During the course of it the Germans had expended more of their strength than they could afford in their straitened circumstances. That expenditure forfeited the chance of maintaining any prolonged resistance to a resumed Allied offensive. . . . In brief, it was Germany's declaration of military bankruptcy."[147]

Opening gaps in one's front by counterattacks is one way of being defeated in a frontal assault. There is also another way and that is to *turn the front into a flank or into a rear.* In other words, when attacked, the army swings around some fixed point, so that the front is no longer perpendicular to the line of communication but parallel to it. In such a position, when the army is parallel to its line of communication, the troops can flee without having to turn on their heels. There is also no need for the army to be scattered, since it faces the line of communication along its entire front.

This method of defeat, though not as popular as the frontal coun-

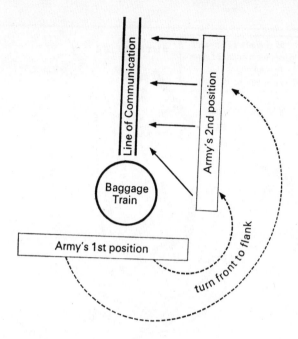

terattack, is quite common. The French army under Marshal
Villeroi was thus defeated by the Duke of Marlborough at the battle of Ramillies in 1706.

When the battle commenced, Villeroi did not open gaps by counterattacks but ordered his troops to retreat in a wheel, like a clos-
ing door (see map), with the left wing at Offus as its hinge. When
the right wing reached Geest, the French army was facing its line of
communication and everyone took immediately to his heels.[148]

A similar method of defeat was employed by the British in the
Second World War. When the Germans attacked France on 10 May
1940, the Allied forces along the Belgian border were facing the
enemy while their back was to their line of communication, which

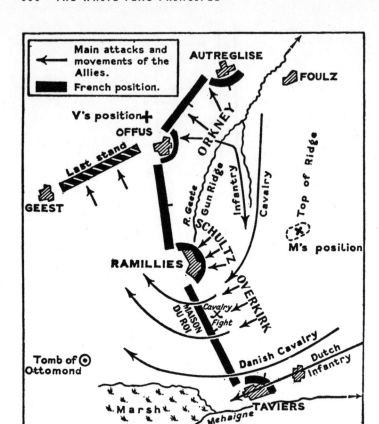

Battle of Ramillies

was—for the British at least—the Channel. Instead of letting the Germans break through gaps, the British forces retreated in a swing until they reached the coastline (see map). Here they stood with their front to the Channel and their back to the enemy, waiting for the boats to take them home.[149]

When troops are attacked not in their front but in their flank,

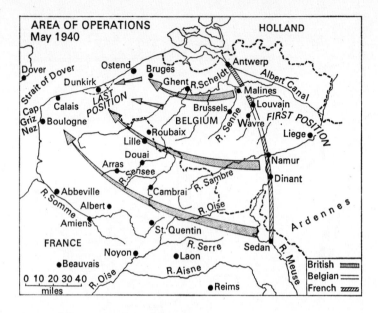

Area of Operations, 30 May 1940

there is no need for such complicated maneuvers. As only the flanks are attacked, the rest of the army can flee without being molested by the enemy or hindered by their own baggage train. It must be remembered that when soldiers are attacked in the flank, they only have to make a half turn in order to present their back to the enemy and not a full turn as they have to do when attacked frontally. For the same reason, a defeat from the rear is the simplest of all defeats since there is no need to make a turn at all. When an army is attacked from the rear, the soldiers' backs are already facing the enemy.

An example of a battle in which an army was defeated by a flank attack is the famous battle at Leuthen on 5 December 1757, when

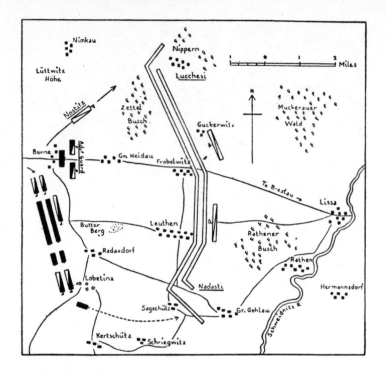

Battle of Leuthen, 5 December 1757

the French army under Prince Charles and Marshal Daun was defeated by Frederick the Great (see map).[150]

A famous battle in which an army was defeated in rear is described in detail by Polybius (Book XI, 1.14-12). This was a battle in Spain in 204 B.C., when Hasdrubal was routed by Marcellus.

Strategy and Tactics of Surrender

The strategy and the tactics of surrender are not based on the principle of flight from the battlefield, but on the principle of the army *staying where it is.* The act of surrender—hoisting a white flag or holding the hands above the head—cannot be performed comfortably on the move. In order to surrender, the soldiers must halt and face the enemy so that they can communicate their intention of surrendering (see Chapter 8).

Though an army can surrender in any given position, it is a great advantage if it surrenders when it is besieged. In a state of siege - and by this we mean not only proper sieges in fortified or natural strongholds but any circular order of battle in which an army is surrounded by the enemy—the army is protected from being out-surrendered by its opponent. The special advantage of the siege is that while the besieged can surrender to the besiegers, the besiegers cannot surrender to the besieged. The besiegers can maintain or lift the siege, but they cannot, under any circumstances, surrender to the besieged.

An army aiming to surrender must make every effort to besiege itself. This can easily be done when the enemy is on the offensive. When the enemy is on the defensive, the surrendering army must assume the offensive and draw the enemy into battle. This having been done, two tactical moves have to be carried out simultaneously: the center holds its ground or even advances; while the wings give way and retreat without breaking formations. If the wings gradually retreat, they meet eventually in the rear. In this way the straight, linear front coils and becomes circular.

A famous battle in which an army besieged itself in the way described is the battle of Cannae, in Italy, in 216 B.C., when the Roman army under Varro and Paulus was encircled by Hannibal.[151] General Fuller described thus the Roman disaster:

> Hannibal with his left wing cavalry charged and routed the Roman right wing cavalry. Then, chasing the Roman left wing

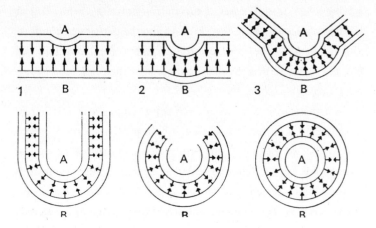

cavalry from the field, as the Roman infantry advanced, he formed his central divisions into a convex formation bulging towards his enemy. Forthwith this crescent was attacked and slowly driven back, until it became concave or hollow-shaped. Into this pocket Varro crowded his men. Suddenly, Hannibal advanced his two divisions of African infantry and wheeling them inwards closed on the Roman flanks. Thereupon the Carthaginian cavalry, returning from the pursuit, fell upon the Roman rear. Thus was Varro's army swallowed up as if by an earthquake.[152]

The battle of Cannae is a brilliant example of surrender tactics. If Varro had been more consistent in his strategy and had surrendered the moment he was encircled, the Roman army could have been saved. As it happened, the Romans changed their minds after they had been encircled and, instead of surrendering, tried to flee from the battlefield. This was a violation of the logic of warfare, which states that defeat cannot follow surrender (see chapter 7). However, for the purpose of military disaster this transgression of the logic of warfare does not matter, since the annihilation of one's army makes the disaster even

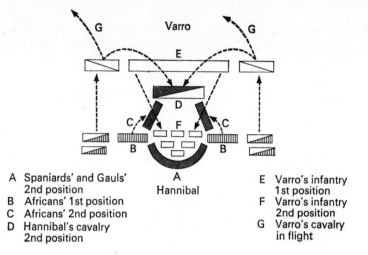

A Spaniards' and Gauls' 2nd position
B Africans' 1st position
C Africans' 2nd position
D Hannibal's cavalry 2nd position

A Hannibal

E Varro's infantry 1st position
F Varro's infantry 2nd position
G Varro's cavalry in flight

more profound. Perhaps one should point out that the complete annihilation of the Roman army at Cannae did Rome no harm at all. On the contrary, it was a débâcle that made Rome a world power for centuries to come.[153]

Examples similar to Cannae can be found in many wars. The Germans, in the Second World War, could have been spared the annihilation of their army at Stalingrad had they fled before they had been surrounded. However, they tried to flee after they were surrounded and, as a result, many of them perished. Nevertheless, their commander, Field Marshal Paulus, did surrender, and so he spent his remaining days in the comfort of a POW camp.

Though surrender is made easier with the aid of a planned strategy and appropriate tactics, it still depends on the correct use of the means by which the desire to surrender is communicated to the enemy. This will be dealt with in the next chapter.

EIGHT

Giving Oneself Up

GIVING ONESELF UP IS THE MOST difficult operation in war. It is even more difficult than the execution of retreat. "Lack of sufficient universal signs of surrender," says Herbert C. Fooks,

causes misunderstandings and failure to make quarter. During the Russo-Japanese War useless casualties occurred for such reason. On 15 June 1904, in the battle of Telis-se about thirty Russians were caught in a house when its roof caught fire. One Russian ran out suddenly unarmed. The Japanese soldiers thought he wished to surrender and approached the building, but were fired upon by another Russian and wounded. A few minutes later another unarmed enemy came out of the building, this time with the purpose of surrendering. The roof was about to fall in on the soldiers within the building and they hoisted a white flag above the door and gave the Russian hand signal for 'Come here,' which meant 'Go away' in Japanese. The Russians stood still and waited while the Japanese undertook to approach and fire upon them. . . . Another time two armies were upon the banks of the Cha-ho, and a Japanese soldier who was on sentry duty saw a Russian soldier throw himself toward him as if he wished to kiss his cheek. The Japanese soldier was ignorant of this expression of sympathy and kept the Russian away with his bayonet. The latter fled but returned within a few minutes and grasped, with effusion, the hand of the Japanese soldier, who understood this time that he desired to surrender.[154]

To make surrender easy and safe, the rules of giving oneself up must be made clear and simple so that even stupid and illiterate soldiers will be able to understand them. After studying all the surrender methods, it has been found that, apart from the old Russian custom of kissing the enemy's cheek, there are no more than two ways by which one can successfully give himself up: one is by hoisting a white flag and the other by raising hands above head. These can be regarded as *visual tokens* of surrender. Nonvisual tokens, such as radio or television broadcasts, are intended to communicate surrender not to the enemy but to one's own people.

The Japanese Emperor's declaration of surrender, broadcast on 15 August 1945, for example, was directed not at the Allied forces but at the Japanese people. On the basis of this broadcast, Japanese soldiers were instructed to give themselves up to the Allied forces in the traditional visual way—by hoisting a white flag or holding up their hands.

It is not accidental that there are two different modes of surrender, since each serves a different purpose. The white flag is the *strategic* token of surrender; one such flag is sufficient for the surrender of a whole army whatever its size. Surrender with hands up is *tactical*; it serves only individual soldiers. It is a well-established military maxim that no more than one soldier can surrender under one pair of raised hands.

Although nothing prevents an army from using hands-up surrender even for strategic purposes, there is no point in ordering a whole army to raise its hands when one white flag is sufficient. On the other hand, the use of a white flag for tactical purposes, that is, for the surrender of an individual soldier, is not uncommon, but it is not sufficient; hands must be raised as well. When individual soldiers surrender only with a white flag, the enemy's acknowledgment of the surrender cannot be known for certain.

Grant Wolfkill records an individual surrender in which only a white flag was used. When the flag was hoisted, Wolfkill remarks, the enemy's gunfire "remained steady." It was only at the second try that "the gunfire reduced. Slowly. From a trickle to drops, isolated shots."[155]

If Wolfkill and his comrades had come out of their hiding place with their hands up, as they should have been done, hostilities would have ceased immediately. With a white flag alone, a tactical surrender (though theoretically possible) is a dangerous operation.

The difference between the two modes of surrender has another, more important application than just to hasten the surrendering process. It happens quite frequently that the victor is not ready to take a whole army into captivity; he might not have enough camps, bedding, equipment or provisions. In such a situation it will be unwise for the vanquished to employ the strategic mode of surrender and send the whole army into captivity by hoisting a white flag.

The surrender of an entire army under a white flag will cause unnecessary hardship. Captives will suffer from lack of accommodation, lack of food and even lack of proper treatment, since there might not be enough wardens to guard them. In the Napoleonic Wars, the British were confronted with this very dilemma. Michael Lewis writes in *Napoleon and His British Captives* that "from 1805 up to the very end, demand [for POW accommodation] invariably exceeded supply. Even at Dartmoor and Perth, all accommodation was earmarked before they were opened. And still the flood rolled in, until the grotesque point was reached at which the government had to order its generals to send no more prisoners home—an order so odd as not always to be obeyed. In 1811–12, for instance, an incredulous Duke of Wellington sent over 20,000 more when expressly told not to do so."[156] In the American Civil War in 1861–65, the captured soldiers—on both sides—suffered hardship because neither side was ready for so many captives within such a short space of time. When the enemy is not ready for a great number of captives, it is better to surrender tactically and go into captivity one by one with hands up, giving the enemy time to build camps, order beds, collect blankets, and so on. The wholesale surrender of the British army in Southeast Asia in 1941 created just such difficulties. While the British surrendered strategically, German and Japanese soldiers submitted *tactically*, one by one, by holding their hands up. Hence their conditions in captivity were much better than the conditions of British soldiers in Japanese camps.

Hoisting a White Flag

It is difficult to say precisely how and when the while flag became the symbol of surrender.[157] It is known, however, that when Cortez discovered Mexico in 1518, he was welcomed by the natives "carrying long poles with a white cotton flag on the end of each. . . ."[158] The white flag, so it seems, has come down to us from ancient times. Moreover, it seems to have been invented or discovered independently in separate and distinct civilizations.

What is really important for the purpose of surrender—so people thought—is not so much the shape or material of the flag as its color. It is known that in many instances any scrap of white or even off-white has been used. Though in use for generations, this practice has been condemned because it creates confusion. What surrendering soldiers have, on occasion, considered to be a white flag has not always been considered so by the enemy. The use of "white" rags—pants, knickers and shirts—has caused miscalculations and misfortunes. In spite of such a "do-it-yourself" white flag, it has happened that the enemy has not ceased firing because he was unable to see or recognize the "thing" which the opponent had been hoisting. Surrender must be carried through in an orderly way, hence it is dangerous to use amateurish substitutes. Every army must equip itself with regulation white flags and hoist them properly.

A regulation surrender white flag is a conspicuous flag, easily recognized by the enemy. In the construction of such a flag, the factors that make it conspicuous must be considered. These are three in number: the flag itself (shape, color and size); the distance between the flag and the enemy; and the weather conditions.

A white flag—like any other regulation flag—can be in one of four possible shapes: it can be *rectangular, triangular, swallow-tailed* or *pendant* (or *pennant*).

The most conspicuous flag is the one that provides the largest surface area for any given breadth and length. Since a rectangular

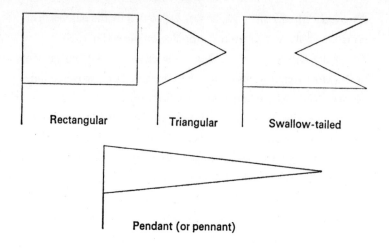

shape provides the largest surface area, this is the recommended shape for a regulation flag. The correct shade of white for surrender purposes is not easy to establish, since many nonwhite colors appear white when they are exposed on a dark background. It is recommended, therefore, to use only an approved white for surrender flags. In Britain there are two approved whites. One is the designated BCC1 (British Colour Council official white) and the other is the British Admiralty bunting pattern designated T-819 for flags made of wool, or T-1145 for flags made of worsted nylon. In other countries similar approved whites can be found.

The size of the rectangular white flag is also difficult to establish because the apparent size depends on the distance between the flag and the enemy. The farther away the enemy, the bigger the flag must be. As there is a limit to the size of a flag that can be comfortably carried, there are other ways—apart from size—of making a white flag conspicuous. Before we discuss them, the rectangular white flag has to be described in more detail.

Though a white flag must be all of one shade, it is still custom-

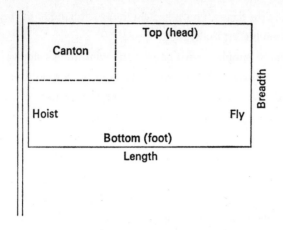

ary to divide it into five parts. There are two horizontal and two vertical divisions. The horizontal is between the *hoist* and the *fly*, while the vertical is between the top or head and bottom or foot. The corner between the hoist and the top is known as the *canton*.[159]

To make a flag sufficiently conspicuous, its full surface must be exposed. This is done by allowing the flag to blow freely in the wind. Therefore, the fabric from which the flag is made must be light. Fabrics like silk, calico and cotton are preferable to velvet, corduroy or tweed. Synthetic light fabrics—nylon, rayon or Dacron —can successfully replace traditional natural materials. It is important to have two kinds of flags always ready; one made of bunting for everyday use and one of silk for ceremonial purposes.

Flags made of light fabrics blow freely in the wind provided that they are carried properly; that is, the flag must be "flying from a staff held by the right hand of the bearer who is facing the observer [the enemy], with the flag flying over the head of the bearer towards his left. That side of the flag which faces the observer is called the 'obverse' and the other side is called the 'reverse.' . . . When dealing with flags of Arabic nations and others who write from right to left . . . the flagstaff must be held in the left hand of the bearer and fly from his left to the right."[160]

This is simple, provided that the wind blows sideways in the desired direction. If the wind blows in the wrong direction—or, worse, if it does not blow at all—the bearer must swing the flag sideways in order to show its obverse or reverse to the enemy. As a flag in motion is more conspicuous than a stationary one, the efficiency of a white flag is thus increased without any change in its size.

Weather conditions other than wind also have a bearing upon the functionality of a white flag. Storm, rain, hail and fog decrease perception and thus conspicuousness and efficiency. It is important, therefore, not to surrender on rainy days but to do so in fine weather. For the same reasons it is useless to hoist a white flag at night, unless the flag is made of or covered with fluorescent material that shines in the dark. Snow also has a neutralizing effect on white flags of surrender, because the flag tends to merge with the white background. It may well be that Napoleon's army in Russia persisted in retreating, instead of submitting—an action which would have saved many lives—because the white covering of the Russian winter made surrender difficult, if not impossible.

Since white flags merge with a snowy background, war is impossible for the Eskimo; they are indeed the only people on earth without warfare. The Antarctic also has been saved from war for the same reasons, although many nations claim parts of its territory. Snow, and the difficulty of surrender in it, may also explain why major war operations usually start in the spring or summer and not in the autumn or winter.[161]

When a proper white flag is not available, an improvised one can be made out of available national flags. The Israeli flag, for example, can easily be turned into a white flag by removing the two blue strips and the Star of David. The Japanese flag can be made completely white by removing the red disc in the middle. It may happen though that by removing the unnecessary colors the flag will become too small or will have holes in it. In such cases, two, three or more flags must be joined together to make one perfect regulation white flag.

How to Make One White Flag Out of Five U.S. National Flags

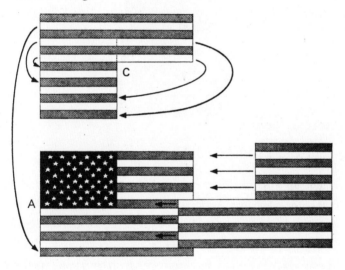

The white stripes of two U.S. flags (C) and (B) can replace the red stripes and the canton of flag (A) and still leave half a white stripe for further use. As every flag has two sides—observe and reverse— two more flags are required for the other side, making five necessary altogether.

Surrender with Hands Up

Hands-up surrender does not involve the use of artifacts as does that of the white flag. Artifacts are, in fact, an obstacle to this mode of surrender, which demands the unhindered use of both hands.

After the soldier has thrown away his weapons, he stands at ease or walks slowly toward the enemy with both his hands raised in the air with the palms flat open facing the enemy. (No closed fists are allowed in hands-up surrender, since they may conceal weapons.)[162] In a proper hands-up posture, the arms are bent in a trident position, forming two right angles: one at the elbow (between the upper and the forearm) and the other at the armpit (between the upper arm and the trunk).

When the enemy is within fifteen to twelve feet (five to four meters) the soldier halts and lifts his arms still higher, until the elbows are level with the top of his head. In this position the climax of surrender is reached. Every movement or emotion must be frozen for a minute or two. If nothing happens in this interval, the surrender can be regarded as successful. The soldier may relax now, though whether he may put down his hands or not depends entirely on his captors, since all responsibility for his future actions is shifted thenceforward to them.[163]

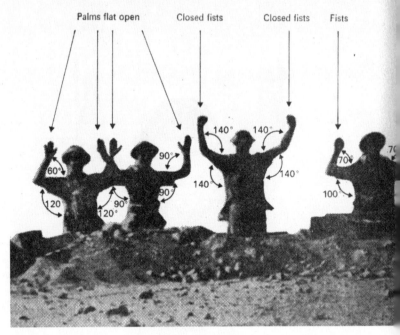

Correct and incorrect surrender postures in the field. Italian soldiers surrendering to the British at Tobruk, in the Western Desert, in January, 1941

The surrender technique described applies only to open country where the enemy is constantly in sight. In closed country—urban, bush or woodland areas—where there is no clear view of the horizon and the enemy may approach unnoticed, soldiers should not abandon their weapons and raise their hands but find shelter and wait in hiding for the enemy. When the enemy arrives, they should leave their weapons in the shelter and come out from their hiding place one by one, with their hands up, as previously described. In

Palms flat open

order not to startle the enemy by a sudden appearance, a small
white flag must be hung beforehand on the exit of the hiding place.

Field Marshal Viscount Slim described thus the surrender of
some Turkish troops in Mesopotamia in the First World War:

> A dirty flag fluttered over the barricade. A swarthy, bearded man
> in bedraggled khaki stepped out with his hands above the head.
> Another followed him, another and another.[164]

CHAPTER NINE

How to Recover from an Accidental Victory

ALTHOUGH THE WHITE FLAG PRINCIPLE is a fault-less principle, we still have to take into account that an army that wanted to be defeated and fulfilled all the necessary requirements for a glorious débâcle could end up not only with a draw, but with a victory. Such a calamity could only occur if the enemy was not only eager to be defeated but managed to fulfil the necessary requisites better and faster.

Since this military manual claims not only to be complete but also to be absolutely perfect, we must cover for such a situation and give clear instructions about how to recover from such a calamity.

Let us start by declaring what not to do:

We ought to know that a war does not usually start with gunpowder. Shooting, bombing, laying mines or using weapons of mass destruction are things that develop later on. Hostilities start in what is known as War Cry Mode. It is a form of warfare that consists of verbal abuse, spoken or written, through the media or the arts. It is known as psychological warfare. Psychological warfare has a double purpose: a) to frighten and soften the enemy, and, at the same time, b) to arouse one's own peoples hatred so as to make them ready for self-sacrifice. This psychological warfare could be compared to barking. We bark at the enemy, belittle him, insult him, smear him with mud, level all sorts of accusations against him, threaten to annihilate him, throw him into the sea, and so on and so forth. People may think that in order to lose a war, we ought to start a similar campaign but in reverse: to praise the enemy, to bless him, to wish him a long life. Nothing could be further from the truth. That is exactly what one should never do. If the enemy will suspect that all you want is a débâcle, he might undo you and raise the white flag himself.

Now that we know what not to do, we can start to discern what has to be done. If we have gone to war in order to be defeated, but ended up victorious, we have to examine the reasons for why we ended up on top. We already know that victory doesn't depend on us (see Chapter 3). It is the defeat of the enemy that made us victorious. We have to examine how the enemy managed to be defeated. If the enemy has been defeated by running away from the battlefield, this is a certain way of being victorious, a corresponding way of recovering from it. If the enemy was defeated by surrender, that is, by raising the white flag, then there is a specific way of recovering from such a victory.

The principle of recovering from a victory can remind us, in a way, of the homeopathic principle of curing a medical disease. The homeopathic principle in medicine is that the poison that made us ill in the first place contains the cure for our recovery. The principle of recovering from victory is the exact opposite of the homeopathic principle in medicine. Our principle states: If you have been victorious because your enemy has been defeated by running away from the battlefield, you ought to surrender by raising the white flag. If you have been victorious because your enemy surrendered by raising the white flag, you can still be defeated if you retreat—that is, if you run away from the battlefield.

It is worthwhile to take a short lesson from Saddam Hussein. We know that he went into the 1990 Gulf War to lose, not win. How do we know this? Simple: if the Iraqis did not manage to overcome the Iranian Army in eight years of war, what chance did they stand against the United States, which has the mightiest army in the world and was also joined by the British, the French and (tacitly) the Russians? Even if we accept the popular notion that Saddam Hussein is crazy, he couldn't have been that crazy. Hussein knew the White Flag Principle[165] and therefore all he wanted to do was to lose and be taken over by the United States, which would cure the terrible economic and social woes of his country. If this was his intention, there was no point in declaring a wish to be defeated. On the contrary, Saddam boasted that he was going to defeat the American, British and French armies, kill their soldiers and send them back in wooden coffins (he never told us how he would get the necessary timber).

When Saddam Hussein surrendered and accepted the allied demands, the Americans became anxious and immediately changed their strategy. Instead of continuing the war, which would have been easy for them to do, they stopped bombing, ceased hostilities, and retreated promptly. If that wasn't "running away from the battlefield," I don't know what is. By retreating the allies robbed Hussein of all the advantages of defeat, and he was not lying or cheating when he claimed in his speeches to the Iraqi people that he was the winner in the battle of the mother of all battles. It took Saddam Hussein some years to realise the misery caused by his victory. (That is why he is now planning another war and hopes for a real defeat afterwards.)

Since there are not many examples of accidental victories, I take the liberty of hypothesizing about what could have happened if the victors of one war had taken preventive actions to turn their victories into defeats in the ways we are suggesting.

Israel won the Six Day War in 1967 because the Arab armies were defeated and ran away from the battlefields. The Syrian Army retreated in panic from the Golan Heights; the Jordanian Army retreated from Jerusalem and the West Bank; and the Egyptian Army retreated from the Gaza Strip and from the Sinai Peninsula. What was the Israeli reaction? There was none. It was later reported that Moshe Dayan, the Minister of Defence, sat next to his telephone and waited for the Arabs to ring him. Nobody rang. I don't have to tell you what the results were. We read about the results in the newspapers, hear about them on the radio and see them on television almost every day. If the Israeli government had a bit of common sense, they would have raised the white flag and surrendered unconditionally to the Arabs the moment they had defeated them. Let us imagine what would have happened if they had done so:

If, on the eve of its victory, Israel had surrendered unconditionally to the Arabs by raising the white flag, the Arabs would have had to negotiate the terms of the surrender with Israel. The mere fact of coming and sitting together implies recognition. The Arabs would have, at last, recognized the existence of the Jewish State, which was Israel's deepest wish from the day it was established.

Now, sitting together and dictating to Israel the terms of the surrender, what could the Arabs have demanded? What kind of conditions could they have dictated to Israel? They couldn't have asked the Jews to jump into the sea. (This was never a practical demand. It was only barking, the part of the psychological warfare that I mentioned before). They couldn't even have demanded that Israel be disarmed because the Arab armies had been destroyed in the fighting and there wasn't a military force to supervise the Israeli Army's disarmament. All the Arabs could have demanded were some minor political concessions like the return of the refugees or some monetary compensation, and by fulfilling these demands Israel could have signed a peace treaty. With a peace treaty the Arabs would have lifted the economic boycott, opened the borders for commerce and tourism, and with Israel's technology, brains and commercial skill, within ten years or even less, Israel would have ruled the whole of the Middle East.

It sounds simple, but it isn't. If your enemy has been defeated and you are surrendering, to whom are you surrendering? If the enemy runs away from the battlefield, and we have already made it clear that the fleeing enemy is always faster than you are, how are you going to catch up with him (if you know where he is!) to let him know that you have surrendered? In ancient times this was very difficult, if not impossible, but now, in modern times, you can send a fax or an email.[166]

If it is difficult to surrender to an enemy who has been defeated, it's much less difficult to be defeated by an army that has surrendered. If the enemy has been defeated and raised the white flag, don't wait until the flag spreads out and expands by the blowing wind. The moment you see the edge of the pole of the white flag rising above the horizon, throw away your weapons and run like mad.

To sum up: there is no way to recover from an accidental victory by surrendering to an army that has already surrendered or being defeated by an army that has already been routed. If the two armies are facing each other and waving white flags, the outcome should be declared a draw. If the two armies are running away from each other in opposite directions, it is a draw as well.

In the rare case of an accidental victory, keep cool and remember this simple rule of thumb: if the enemy runs away—raise the white flag; if the enemy raises the white flag—run.

TEN

The March into Captivity

THE SOLDIER WHO HAS GIVEN himself up has made a contribution to the military *débâcle* of his army. Whether his surrender has actually caused the army's collapse is immaterial. As far as the soldier himself is concerned, he has done his duty and is entitled to gather the rewards of surrender?

What are the rewards of surrender?

Since the fruits of fighting are mortal danger, hardships and humiliation, we expect the rewards of surrender to be security, pleasure and respect. With some exceptions, which will be dealt with later, these are indeed the conditions of captivity. To begin with, the captor must take his prisoners of war out of the fighting zone, to save them from any hazard to their life.[167] In the Second World War, out of 235,473 British and American POWs in Germany and Italy, only 9,348 died—a mere four percent. This is a smaller percentage than that of soldiers who die in combat, and not much more than that of people dying in peace time.

Apart from saving his captive's life, the enemy satisfies all his worldly needs. He provides him with shelter, clothing, food, physical and intellectual facilities, entertainment and so forth.[168] Prisoners of war are, on the whole, more respected than free, fighting soldiers. This is custom as well as law.[169] H. C. W. Bishop, one of the captives when the British Expeditionary Force in Mesopotamia surrendered to the Turks in 1916, tells how "An Indian sweeper— the humblest of all regimental followers—was trudging along behind his regiment carrying some of the articles of his trade, when they passed some Turkish gunpits where there were several German officers standing. On seeing them the sweeper made obeisance with the deepest of salaams; whereupon the Germans promptly stood to attention, clicked their heels and saluted."[170]

The favors bestowed on prisoners of war are not limited to bare essentials or matters of honor. Red Cross parcels, for example, are luxuries which no free, fighting man has ever received. POWs are also exempt from port, customs and other duties.[171] They have extraordinary travel opportunities. Many British prisoners taken by the Japanese in Malaya, in 1941, traveled through Burma, Siam, Indochina, China, Manchuria and Japan, without having to fight their way, as other British soldiers were to do two years later. It is difficult for an American citizen to travel to North Korea unless he is a prisoner of war, and until recently, Cuba and Vietnam were off-limits as well. It is also important to point out that a POW is never "forgotten" as is the fighting man in the trenches. The POW is a focus of world attention, pity and sympathy. Representatives of neutral countries never visit soldiers as they do prisoners of war. If something is not to the POW's complete satisfaction he can complain and send out petitions.[172] A free soldier cannot send out petitions, and his right to complain is very restricted.

Life in captivity is good. It is especially good when compared with the life of a "free" soldier in the fighting army.[173]

However, it must be admitted that few POWs take advantage of their opportunities. Though some enjoy their life in captivity, many do not. A study of prison life reveals that there are two common causes for the captive's dissatisfaction: one is fear of the enemy's treatment and the other is *barbed wire disease*.

The excellent conditions of captivity are greatly resented by traditional armies. They fear that if soldiers were to know about the conditions in captivity, they would give themselves up on the first opportunity. To prevent troops from surrendering, the truth about life in captivity is suppressed and replaced by a falsification that describes the conditions of life in captivity as unendurable. "Slander of the enemy," says Arthur Ponsonby, "is esteemed a patriotic duty . . . stories of maltreatment of prisoners have to be circulated deliberately in order to prevent surrenders. This is done of course on both sides. Whereas naturally each side tries to treat its prisoners as well as possible so as to attract others."[174] Similar views have been expressed by other military historians like Daniel J. McCarthy and General J. F. C. Fuller.[175]

It is not surprising, therefore, that, after the initial relief that soldiers experience when their surrender has been successfully carried through, they may be gripped with fear and anxiety.[176] In such a mood, happiness is obviously out of the question. Every action carried out by the enemy is interpreted as an act of cruelty, neglect or humiliation. Karl Nork, a German soldier in Russian captivity in the Second World War, tells how the Russians picked out German soldiers with military decorations and ordered them to dig a deep trench. Nork records that all the POWs were terrified, since they were sure that these were their forthcoming graves. It was only in the evening that they discovered that the trench was merely intended for the POWs' own good: it was to be a latrine.[177]

There are many instances of this kind; they show that what really spoils the enjoyment of captivity is not the enemy's maltreatment—for there is little—but the expectation of such maltreatment. In order to make its soldiers march into captivity in a mood of elation instead of resentment, the captive army must not indulge in patriotic propaganda of the sort just described. Instead, it must reveal the truth. It must be made clear to the troops that their chances of being maltreated in captivity are negligible and can, therefore, be ignored. Generous treatment of POWs is not just a modern humanistic trend created by the international war-conventions of the twentieth century. Generous treatment of POWs is a very ancient custom. As far back as the first century B.C., soldiers who gave themselves up to the Chinese were rewarded by the Emperor Wu with gifts and money. Ssu-ma Ch'ien, the Grand Historian of China, records that when the Hsung-nu surrendered, the Emperor offered them "rewards amounting to a billion cash."[178] When it once happened that the funds in the district offices were not enough to pay the rewards the emperor was obliged to "reduce the expenses of his own table, dispense with the carriage drawn by four horses of matched colour, and pay out money from his private reserves in order to make up the deficiency."[179]

The Romans were not so generous as the Chinese, but there was nothing in their treatment of POWs that was humiliating. This can be deduced from Cicero's comment: "It is our duty not only to be merciful to the conquered, but . . . to shelter those who lay down their arms. . . ."[180] This was the Roman attitude not only during the

republic but also during the heyday of the empire. Gibbon mentions that the Empress Zenobia went into "exile" in a splendid villa at Tivoli, where she "sunk into a Roman matron and her daughters married into the most noble families."[181] The Gaulish king Tetricus was awarded (for his surrender) the governorship of Lucania; Gibbon quotes the Roman Emperor Aurelian as asking the vanquished king if "it were not more desirable to administer a province in Italy than to reign beyond the Alps?"[182]

That the custom of treating POWs generously is universal can be seen from the paintings on certain ancient Peruvian pottery vessels of the Fluorescent (Mocha) period (A.D. 200-600), in which captives can be seen to be carried in litters.[183] Many examples testify that generous treatment of prisoners of war was the rule more than the exception in ancient as well as in more recent times. Emmerich de Vattel summed up the treatment of prisoners of war in his time (the eighteenth century) as follows: "Let us, in this particular, bestow on the European nations the praise to which they are justly entitled. Prisoners of war are seldom ill-treated among them. We extol the English and the French; we feel our bosom glow with love for them, when we hear the accounts of the treatment which prisoners of war, on both sides, have experienced from these generous nations."[184]

The First and Second World Wars offer us innumerable examples

that do not differ from those of ancient times. Mr. Lithgow
Osborne, in an address to the British Parliament in 1916, confirmed
the excellent conditions in prison camps in Germany, with the
exception of one, that in Wittenberg, in which the conditions of
prisoners of war were less satisfactory.[185] Though many publications during 1914-19 often accused the enemy of maltreatment of
prisoners, they belonged to the sort of propaganda mentioned ear-
lier. In a recent book dealing with the surrender of the British Expeditionary Force in Kut, in 1916, the fate of the POWs marching
into captivity is described as follows:

> Approaching the white-stone ruins [of Ctesiphon] was a long,
> straggling column of some 2,000 British soldiers. Some still wore
> the remains of khaki drill tropical uniform; others were almost
> naked. They had stumbled and staggered for nearly fifteen miles
> that day without water or food. The suffocating heat had reduced
> the men to the point where brains were numb and eyes had taken
> on the blank stare of the hopeless. The wake of the column was
> strewn with human litter, the dead, the dying and others, unable
> to march any further, waiting for death from the rise butts of their
> Arab guards.[186]

It is an appalling description indeed. However, in the memoirs
of the captives themselves, published shortly after the armistice,
a rather different picture emerges. H. C. W. Bishop tells how generous the Turks were, paying the prisoners their salary in gold
instead of the banknotes that nobody honored. The prisoners
were allowed to bathe in the river during the march in the hot
desert; they were allowed to visit the nearby towns and once
they were invited by the Turkish commander to a coffeehouse.[187]
There is no mention of molestation by the Turkish guards.

Major C.H. Barber, also a captive, tells a similar story. Among other things, Barber describes a visit to the British wounded prisoners in a hospital in Baghdad:

> The officers were in a small ward which was clean and bright, and which they shared with some Turks. . . . They said the Turks treated them well . . . the men were in a larger general ward, and seemed to be treated in the same way as the Turkish soldiers, and to be more or less contented.[188]

The lot of POWs in the Second World War was no less fortunate than their lot in the first. When Anthony Deane-Drummond, a POW in Solmone, in Italy, tried to persuade his comrades to join him in escape, they answered that "they did not want to escape, they saw no point in it and if ever a tunnel was built and if they were ordered to get out through it, they would start building another one now, through which to get back inside the camp again. . . . "[189]

Italy was not the only country where POWs had such a good time that they ignored and rejected opportunities of escaping. Wing Commander H. Day, one of the most famous British POWs in Nazi Germany, spent many a night feasting and dining with Rumpel, the German commander of his prison. The description of these lavish dinner parties fills one with envy: "It was a hilarious evening. . . . The Rhine wine flowed and the hospitality only ceased when the host retired, literally, under the table, telling them [the POWs] to find their way back to prison. They did . . . and then had to argue with the sentry on the gate before he would let them into the camp."[190]

Studying the memoirs of ex-POWs in the Second World War, one wonders what the source was of all the reported cases of maltreatment. It would be tedious indeed to quote all the available evidence

A TABLE CHART OF DAILY FOOD RATIONS IN COLDITZ

Day	Breakfast	gr.	Lunch	gr.	Dinner	gr.
Monday	Coffee subst.	4	Potatoes Turnips	400 550	Jam subst. Bread	20 300
Tuesday	Coffee subst.	4	Potatoes Turnips	400 600	Jam subst. Bread	20 300
Wednesday	Coffee subst.	4	Potatoes Turnips	400 500	Jam Bread	20 300
Thursday	Coffee subst.	4	Potatoes Turnips	400 500	Jam subst. Bread	20 300
Friday	Coffee subst.	4	Potatoes	400	Jam subst. Bread Cheese	20 300 $31\frac{1}{4}$
Saturday	Coffee subst.	4	Potatoes Peas Millet Oats Barley Cooking fat	400 $112\frac{1}{2}$ 75 $62\frac{1}{2}$ $37\frac{1}{2}$ 68	Jam subst. Sugar Jam Bread	20 175 175 300
Sunday	Coffee subst.	$3\frac{1}{2}$	Potatoes Fresh meat Turnips	350 250 600	Jam subst. Bread	30 425

to the contrary. However, the conditions at the most heavily guarded prison in Nazi Germany at the time, Colditz, is of some importance, since it was here that chronic escapers were kept. If German treatment of prisoners of war was as barbarous as it was alleged to be, Colditz must have been the place where such treatment was applied. Nothing of the sort is found in the publications of the ex-inmates of Colditz. There is nothing to suggest humiliation, hardship or malnutrition. The prisoners were well fed, well treated and honorably respected. When they were not busy planning or digging their escape, they led a life of leisure: playing, reading, studying and so on. The daily routine in Colditz prison is described by P.R. Reid as follows: "Teachers and pupils paired off and sought out quiet corners all over the castle, where they could settle down to explain to each other the intricacies of the various European languages. Our living room became a hive of industry and the low murmur of voices continued unabated throughout the morning hours. Those who sought more privacy chose to sit on the staircase or on blankets in the lobbies or out in the courtyard, if it was fine."[191] If anything, life in Colditz prison reminds one of life in a well-kept monastery in the Middle Ages. Reid produces a chart of the rations to show that there was no malnutrition in Colditz (see page 134).[192]

In clashes between the United States army and Communist forces in the Far East in the 1960s, allegations of maltreatment of POWs were common. The Communists were especially accused of "brainwashing" their prisoners by means of mental or physical torture. But in a book written by an American and based on information supplied by the U.S. army, such torture is denied: "The techniques by which the Communists [in North Korea] indoctrinated our men were not based on physical force. There is no record in any of the returnees' files of the use of physical force or physical torture as a means of indoctrination."[193] Although this leaves the question of "mental torture" still open, no specific evidence is given. On the contrary, all the evidence indicates that the POWs were most cordially treated.

Fear of the enemy's treatment is the result of conditioning by patriotic propaganda. This makes soldiers anxious and depressed when they march into captivity. When the march is over and the POWs settle in their camps, they see for themselves that their fears were unfounded. They then feel better, but not for long. As soon as they get used to their new, comfortable conditions, they are struck with *barbed wire disease.*

Barbed wire disease is not confined solely to prisoners of war. It occurs also among ships' crews, in hospitals, in monasteries and among explorers.[194] However, it is in captivity that it is most virulent. "The disease manifests itself in a series of symptoms, varying in degree with the individual. Foremost is an increased irritability, so that the patients cannot stand the slightest opposition and readily fly into passion. A mania for discussion develops, but sound judgment is entirely lacking in the argument. In intercourse with others patients are extraordinarily paltry, invariably seeking their own advantage. They find intense difficulty in concentrating on one particular object; their mode of life becomes unstable, and there is a restlessness in all their actions."[195] Among other symptoms of the disease is a pessimistic view of events and a deep depression called by the French *cafard.*[196] It also includes sleeplessness, and eyesight often becomes defective. Some sufferers complain of sexual impotence and inability to engage in intellectual activities.[197]

It is important to point out that the enemy's treatment has but little influence on barbed wire disease. "Cruel, brutal treatment does not produce the disease, neither does good treatment prevent it."[198] Even Napoleon suffered from barbed wire disease, though his conditions on the island of St. Helena were better than those of the best-kept POWs.[199]

Barbed wire disease, so it seems, is not the result of maltreatment, but rather of lack of excitement. It resembles, in many ways, the kind of neurosis that very rich people who lead a life of leisure suffer from. The similarity between rich-man neurosis and barbed wire disease also suggests similar treatment.[200] Since big-game hunting, the usual cure for this type of neurosis, is out of the question for POWs, substitutes have to be prescribed. Fortunately, there is a substitute in prison life which is regarded by experts to be equal if not superior to big-game hunting, and that is *escape*.[201] Escape from prison is superior to big-game hunting not only because it affords more excitement, thrill and suspense, but because it gives the escapees a sense of purpose that makes their life meaningful. It has been observed that when POWs are planning, cutting, sawing or digging their way to freedom, they are not affected by barbed wire disease. The correlation between escape and barbed wire disease— which in extreme cases is fatal—has been statistically confirmed. The rate of death of U.S. soldiers in North Korea's prison camps in the fifties could not be accounted for by malnourishment or hardship, or by any other physical cause. The mystery was solved when it was discovered that the Korean War was the first war in U.S. history in which not a single soldier escaped.[202]

It goes without saying that when one is planning an escape, great care must be taken not to make it too successful. If an escape is entirely successful, the soldier is sent back to the battlefield. When one is already a captive, there is no point in returning to the battlefield as a soldier in order to surrender again. To cure barbed wire disease it is enough to escape from the prison camp, wander into enemy territory and be caught while crossing the border. The closer to the border one is caught, the greater the excitement. There is no reason for an escaped POW to be afraid of being caught. According to international law and the prevailing custom, the punishment for an attempted escape is a limited period of solitary confinement.

Smiling in the front row are (left to right): Göring, Hess, Ribbentrop and Keitel. In the second row are: Doenitz, Raeder, Schirach and Sauckel

On his release from the "cooler," as the solitary confinement cell is popularly known, the captive can immediately start planning a new escape.

So far, we have been discussing the fate of the common prisoner of war: the man whose prospects in captivity are excellent and can be made—with a little effort—even better. However, it must be remembered that there are POWs who are less fortunate. Though they are not worse off than the free, fighting man (none can be worse off than he is), many are certainly no better off. These are the prisoners who suffer humiliation, hardship, torture and sometimes even death.

These wretched POWs deserve special attention. Though they are referred to as belonging all to one group—*prisoners who suffer*—they are, in fact, of two different classes. On the one hand, we have the *war criminals*, those who are put on trial, imprisoned and sometimes executed; on the other, we have the *victims* of these war criminals.

Though suffering is the common denominator of both these kinds, the status of each differs considerably. The war criminals belong to the vanquished, while their victims belong to the victors. Since it is not our intention or duty to heed the victors, the victims of the war criminals are not our concern. Their fate, whatever it is, has no bearing on the life of POWs of the vanquished. From the viewpoint of *The White Flag Principle*, there is only one kind of captive who suffers, and that is the war criminal.

War criminals do suffer in captivity, but only once they are found guilty of their crimes. Until then their lot in prison is far better than that of any other POW who has not committed crimes. When the top Nazi war-criminal, Hermann Göring, was caught, he was fêted by his captors and given cocktail parties in which he made speeches and statements to the press.[203] During their trial, the war criminals were lavishly treated, as is evident from the testimony of the man who was the top Nazi jailer: "As we fed them [the war criminals awaiting trial] with thick soup, beef and vegetables, the internees seemed to thrive, and they began to put on weight, while Göring was taking his excess fat off."[204]

Fifty-two years later, another war criminal was put on trial. Slobodan Milosevic, the former president of Serbia and then of Yugoslavia, was facing 66 counts of war crimes in Croatia, Bosnia and Kosovo, during the violent disintegration of the Yugoslav federation in the 1990s.

During his lengthy trial in the Hague it was discovered that Milo-sevic was so strained by the Court proceedings that he might have suffered a heart attack. It was not Milesovic who complained. It was below his dignity to complain. It was the court itself that was worried about his state of health. It ordered a medical report in June 2002 and a month later, a London-based newspaper, *The Guardian*, reported: "Reviewing progress in the biggest war crimes case since Hitler's henchmen were tried at Nuremberg, Judge May revealed that a report by two Dutch court-appointed doctors had shown 'severe cardiovascular risk' to the accused. 'His workload must be reduced and medical treatment by a cardiologist is most advisable.' The court would 'consider any option that may be avail-able for the future conduct of the trial.'"[205] How fortunate Milo-sevic was to lose the war! If he had been victorious nobody would have been worried. Has there ever been such a consideration for the health of a *victorious* head of state?

There is nothing in the treatment of war criminals—the only van-quished POWs who suffer—that contradicts or invalidates anything that has been so far said about the marvelous life in captivity. This being so, there is no reason for a war criminal not to give himself up. After all, the number of war criminals who have been caught and punished is minute compared with the total number of those who have committed crimes. Even if caught, most of them are never brought to justice. Those who are brought, eventually, to the dock, stand a good chance of being acquitted, since a good war criminal does not leave many witnesses behind. If it so happens that a war criminal is found guilty and sentenced, he still has a chance of being released before his time is up (amnesties are especially common after war). Out of the top Nazi criminals sentenced to life impris-onment by the International War Tribunal at Nuremberg, only one,

Rudolf Hess, remained in prison. All the others have been released one way or another. Even the threat of a death sentence should not deter a war criminal from giving himself up, since the threat does not mean that the sentence will be carried out. If the worst comes to the worst, the POW can still outwit his captors and commit suicide as Göring did. No wonder that the top Nazi war criminals were so cheerful in the courtroom at Nuremberg (see picture).

The suffering of the criminals of war, though sometimes acute, is never as painful or humiliating as is commonly believed.

Life in captivity is so good that when POWs are released and sent back home they find it difficult to adjust to liberty. When the American captives in Korea were released, the U.S. army put them back into prison. Eugene Kinkhead reports that the ex-prisoners of the Korean War "were housed on what had been a Japanese post, and were not to mingle with other members of the armed forces. This was necessary, the Army felt, both from the standpoint of security and for the men's own good, since psychiatrists had advised that the returnees be allowed to become acclimated to freedom gradually."[206]

The release of the POWs and their adjustment to liberty is a serious problem. So the restoration of sovereignty to the vanquished, which comes as soon as the victor realizes the burden he has put on himself by occupying his opponent's territory. These problems, however, are not considered military débâcles in the strict sense and therefore cannot be dealt with in the present volume. As far as military disasters are concerned, our task has been completed with the march of the troops into captivity. The surrender of the troops and their march into captivity demobilizes the army. With the disappearance of the army, all the military problems—including débâcles—cease to exist.

Notes

1. "War—the highest form of struggle in existence . . . for settling contradictions between classes, between nations, between states, or between political groups . . ." Mao Tse-tung, *Strategic Problems of China's Revolutionary War*, Foreign Languages Press, Peking, 1954, p. 2.

2. L. C. Lewin, *Report from Iron Mountain*, Penguin, London, 1967, p. 87. American ed., Dell, New York, 1969.

3. In a speech in the House of Commons, 13 May 1940.

4. Cecil Woodham-Smith, *The Reason Why*, Penguin, London, 1958, p. 9.

5. "Warre consisteth not in Battell onely, or the act of fighting; but in a tract of time, wherein the will to contend by Battell is sufficiently Known; and therefore the notion of time, is to be considered in the nature of Warre; as it is in the nature of Weather." Thomas Hobbes, Leviathan (1651), Dent, London, 1914, Ch. 13.

6. Quoted by B. H. Liddell Hart in *Strategy: The Indirect Approach*, Faber & Faber, London, 1967 ed., p. 63.

7. Ibid., p. 215.

8. Ibid., p. 351. See also J. F. C. Fuller, *The Generalship of Alexander the Great*, Eyre & Spottiswoode, London, 1958, p. 312. "Victory at all costs is strategic humbug."

9. Last note in *On War* by Karl von Clausewitz, ed. Anatol Rapoport, Penguin, London, 1968.

10. J. R. R. Tolkien, *The Hobbit*, Unwin, London, 1970 (l9th imprint), p. 262.

11. Joseph Heller, *Catch-22*, Simon & Schuster, New York, 1961, p. 240.

12. See "Sayings of the Week" in the London *Observer*. 1 September 1968.

13. Alfred H. Burne, *The Art of War on Land*, Methuen, London, 1944, p. 1.

14. See von Clausewitz, *op. cit.* Bk. 1, Ch. 7.

15. Tr. Rex Warner, Penguin, London, 1954, p. 78.

16. "*Graecia capta forum victorem cepit et artes intulit agresti latio.*" *Epistles*, II, i, 156.

17. J. F. C. Fuller, *The Conduct of War*. Eyre & Spottiswoode, London, 1962, p. 13.

18. *Ibn Jubayr Travells*, tr. from Arabic by S. M., Beirut House Publishers, 1984, pp. 274-75.

19. Tr. G. A. Williamson, Penguin, London, 1966. See Ch. 3, "Justinian's Misgovernment".

20. S. Dumas and Vedel Peterson, *Losses of Life Caused by War,* Clarendon Press, Oxford, 1923, p. 119. The reported number of casualties in battle must always be taken with great caution. Even reliable authorities cannot be trusted in this matter. Michailowsky, in *Geschichte des Krieges Russlands mit Frankreich unter der Regierung Kaiser Pauls I im Jahre 1799*, compares the number of French losses in one battle (4 November 1797) as reported by different authorities:

Authority	Killed	Wounded	Prisoners	Missing	Total
Suvaroff	7,000	5,000	4,600	4,000	20,600
Mélas	3,000	4,000	4,000		11,000
Kamavoski	4,500	4,600			9,100
Jomini	1,500	5,000	3,000		9,500

21. J. F. C. Fuller, *Decisive Battles*, Eyre & Spottiswoode, London, 1939, II, p.692

22. S. Dumas and Vedel Peterson, *Losses of Life Caused by War*, Clarendon Press, Oxford, 1923, p. 45.

23. Gaston Bodart, *Losses of Life in Modern War*, Clarendon Press, Oxford, 1916, p. 25.

24. *Ibid.* pp. 30-31.

25. *Ibid.*

26. J. F. C. Fuller, *Decisive Battles*, II, p. 781.

27. *New American Encyclopedia*, 1963. Entry: "Verdun."

28. *Ibid*. Entry: "World War I."

29. Colonel L. P. Ayres, *The War with Germany*, Government Printing Office, Washington, 1919, p. 119.

30. *Encyclopaedia Britannica*. Entry: "World War II."

31. "Some Thracian is pleased with my shield, which unwillingly I left on a bush in perfect condition on our side, but I escaped death. To hell with that shield! I shall get another, no worse." Archilochus (648 B.C.), *The Penguin Book of Greek Verse*, London, 1971, p.129.

32. Lloyd and Tempelhoff, *The History of the Seven Years' War in Germany*, tr. C. H. Smith, War Office, London, 1808, 1, 271.

33. War has many definitions. For example: "Two persons' zero-sum game with no complete information" (Oskar Morgenstern and John von Neumann, *Theory of Games and Economic Behaviour*, Princeton University Press, Princeton, 1947. See Anatol Rapoport, "The Use and Misuse of Game Theory," *Scientific American*, Vol. 207, No. 6, New York, 1962); "A continuation of policy by other means" (Karl von Clausewitz, *On War*, ed. Anatol Rapoport, Penguin, London, 1968); "Not a continuation but a failure of policy" (A. Rapoport); "The trade of kings" (John Dryden); "Any persons, thing, idea, entity or location selected for destruction, inactivation, or rendering nonusable with weapons which will reduce or destroy the will or ability of the enemy to resist" (U.S. Air Force ROTC manual).

34. Karl von Clausewitz, *op. cit.*, p. 101

35. ———, *The Principles of War*, tr. Hilaire Belloc, Chapman & Hall, London, 1918, p. 218

36. ———, *op cit.*, Bk. IV, p. 313.

37. *Ibid.*, p.311

38. Letter dated 6 February 1945. See *The Testament of Adolf Hitler* (the Hitler-Bormann Documents, Feb.-Apr., 1945), tr. R. H. Stevens, Cassell, London, 1959, p.41

39. See General Tojo's conversation with the Japanese war minister Anami in the Pacific War Research Society, *Japan's Longest Day*, Corgi Books, London, 1969, pp. 113-14.

40. Plutarch, *The Rise and Fall of Athens*, tr. Ian Scott-Kilvert, Penguin, London, 1960, p. 215.

41. Marcus Tullius Cicero, Thacydides, *Selected Political Speeches of Cicero*, tr. Michael Grant, Penguin, London, 1969, p.38

42. Thucydides, *History of the Peloponnesian War*, tr. Rex Warner, Penguin, London, 1954, Bk. I, p. 43.

43. Xenophon, *Memoirs of Socrates and the Symposium*, tr. Hugh Tredennick, Penguin, London, 1970, iv. 2. 14-17 (p. 187)

44. Tr. Illinois Greek Club, Loeb Classical Library, Heinemann, London, 1923, vol. XXIII.

45. Charles Oman, *A History of the Art of War*, Methuen, London, 1898, p. 201.

46. Max Weber, *Essays in Sociology*, tr. H. H. Gerth, C. Wright Mills, et al., Routledge & Kegan Paul, London, 1948, p.168.

47. *Arms and the Woman: The Diaries of Baron Boris Uxküll*, 1812-19, ed. Detler von Uexküll, tr. Joel Carmichael, Secker & Warburg, London, 1966, p.107.

48. Anthelme Brillat-Savarin, *The Philosopher in the Kitchen*, tr. Anne Drayton, Penguin, London, 1970, p. 135.

49. *Ibid.*, p. 136

50. Lewis Mumford, *Technics and Civilization*, Routledge, London, 1934, pp. 93-4.

51. Adolf Hitler, *The Testament of Adolf Hitler* (The Hitler-Bormann Documents. Feb.-Apr., 1945), tr. R. H. Stevens, Cassell, London, 1959 p. 43.

52. The National Defense Advisory Commission stated on 30 Decem-

ber 1941 that the nation's arms output was up to 2,400 airplane engines, 700 planes, more than 10,000 semiautomatic rifles and 100 tanks a month. Over a million persons had been put to work in the previous two months by the defense program, and several million more would be needed by the following November. Contracts had been approved for over $10 billion, the Army and Navy being awarded nine-tenths of these, including $3.3 billion for ships, $1.5 billion for factory expansion and housing, $1.5 billion for planes and parts, $500 million for ammunition, $500 million for guns and $400 million for tanks and trucks. These contracts, plus those placed by Britain and other nations, committed American industry to producing 50,000 planes, 130,000 aero-engines, 9,200 tanks, 17,000 heavy guns, 25,000 light guns, 13,000 trench mortars, 300,000 machine guns and ammunition, 400,000 automatic rifles and ammunition, 1.3 million regular rifles and ammunition, 380 navy ships, 200 merchant ships, 210 camps and cantonments, 50 million trucks and clothing and equipment for 1.2 million men. (*Keesing's Contemporary Archives*, 4503; American ed. published by Horizon Press, New York, 1962.)

53. "All history teaches that no enemy is so insignificant as to be despised and neglected by any power, however formidable." Henri Jomini, *Summary of the Art of War*, ed. J. D. Hittle, Military Service Publishing Co., Harrisburg, 1947, p. 46.

54. King Carol of Rumania declared on 15 August 1938 at Constanza: "The determination to defend our frontiers exists as steel-hard faith in the soul of every Rumanian. . . . That which is Rumanian can never be given away. That which is Rumanian will be defended and those who love peace must be aware that frontiers once traced cannot be changed without the danger of a world cataclysm." (*Keesing's Contemporary Archives*, 3689.)

55. A legal document is a document presented by a legal government. In principle, this has nothing to do with the source of the document. Any document presented by a legal government is a legal document. A legal government is a government that can present legal documents.

56. "Frederick II of Prussia, while Austria and France were at war,

brought forward an old claim, in 1744 entered Bohemia in force, and seized this province, thus doubling the power of Prussia." Henri Jomini, *op. cit.*, p. 45.

57. Quotations from *Keesing's Contemporary Archives*, 20927.

58. The friendship between India and China was proclaimed in 1954 by the Pancha Sila, the Five Principles: (1) mutual respect for each other's territorial integrity and sovereignty; (2) nonaggression; (3) noninterference in each other's internal affairs; (4) equality and mutual benefit; (5) peaceful coexistence. From a joint statement issued by Chou En-lai and Nehru on 28 June 1954 (see *Keesing's Contemporary Archives*).

59. Moreover, provoking the enemy by proclaiming his "dangerous intention" may have the effect of a "self-fulfilling prophecy"; the "enemy" will "respond" and in this way actually becomes as dangerous to the group as it accused him of being in the first place. Lewis Coser, *The Functions of Social Conflict*, Routledge & Kegan Paul, London, 1956, pp. 105-6.

60. Accidental claims are employed not only in national but also in regional disputes. On 16 November 1970 the *Times* of London reported that "the transfer of land from Flintshire to Cheshire on the latest Ordnance Survey map has been described as 'common piracy.' . . . According to the map, a large area of marshland, mud flats and water in the Dee estuary which is to be reclaimed for industrial development becomes Cheshire territory. The Welsh boundary, previously in the middle of the estuary, has been moved to the Welsh side."

61. Attacking a country without making it an enemy beforehand was considered a crime even in ancient times. Procopius comments that "The more responsible members of the invading [Persian] army began to protest to Chosroes, accusing him of violating both his own oats and international laws accepted by all nations: in time of peace he had invaded Roman territory entirely without provocation. . . . " (*The Secret History*, tr. G. A. Williamson, Penguin, London, 1966, pp. 50-51. See also Henri Jomini, *op. cit.*, p. 50: "A war of invasion without good reason—like that of Genghis Khan—is a crime against humanity; but," he adds, "it may be excused, if not approved, when induced by great interest or when conducted with good motives."

62. Once a noncontiguous enemy has been made, he can be used to make other noncontiguous enemies.

63. J. F. C. Fuller, *The Conduct of War*, Eyre & Spottiswoode, London, 1962, p. 270.

64. See Sir Winston Churchill, *The Second World War*, Cassell, London, 1951, III, pp. 526-27.

65. U.S. Congress, *Hearings Before the Joint Committee on the Pearl Harbor Attack*, Washington, 1946, Pt. II, p. 5433.

66. "Disappearance of the original enemy leads to a search for new enemies so that the group may continue to engage in conflict, thereby maintaining a structure that it would be in danger of losing were there no longer an enemy." Lewis Coser, *op. cit.*, p. 105.

67. ". . . in most diplomatic and consular establishments abroad espionage agents of the C.I.A. are stationed masquerading as diplomatic and consular officers." (Joachim Joesten, *They Call It Intelligence: Spies and Spy Techniques Since World War II*, Abelard-Schuman, New York, 1963, p. 4.)

68. The monopoly of the United States in getting rid of allies by cordial treatment was traditionally challenged by the Soviet Union. On 19 October 1970 the *Times* of London reported: "After increasingly gearing their industrial development programme to Soviet assistance in recent years, many Indians are beginning to suspect that Russian aid donors and technicians can also be ugly Americans. . . . The Russians themselves are beginning to feel the backlash of criticism which western nations have experienced when aid turns sour."

69. "The great art to make a nation happy, and what we call flourishing, consists in giving everybody an opportunity of being employed; which to compass, let a Government's first care be to promote as great a variety of Manufactures, Arts and Handicrafts as human wit can invent; and the second to encourage Agriculture and Fishery in all their branches, that the whole Earth may exert itself as well as Man. It is from this Policy and not from the trifling regulations of Lavishness and Frugality that the greatness and felicity of Nations must be expected; for let the value of Gold and Silver rise or fall, the enjoyment of all Societies will ever depend upon the Fruits of the Earth and the Labour of the People; both

which joined together are a more certain, a more inexhaustible and a more real treasure than the Gold of Brazil or the Silver of Potosi." (Bernard Mandeville, *The Fable of the Bees* (1723), Penguin, London, 1970.)

70. David Ricardo, *Principles of Political Economy*, Penguin, London, 1971, pp. 107-8.

71. T. R. Malthus *An Essay on the Principle of Population* (1798) Penguin, London, 1970.

72. See also Henry George, *Progress and Poverty*, Robert Shalkenbach Foundation, New York, 1933; Thorstein Veblen, *The Theory of Business Enterprise*, Scribner's, New York, 1932; and Sir Arthur Salter, *Recovery: The Second Effort* ("The defects of the capitalistic system have been increasingly robbing us of its benefits, they are now threatening its existence"), Bell, London, 1934.

73. John Maynard Keynes, *The General Theory of Employment, Interest and Money*, Macmillan, London, 1967, pp. 104-5.

74. While inflation has always been recognized as such, the same cannot be said about deflation. After every deflationary disaster, the name of the calamity is changed. Sometimes it is called *recession*, sometimes *slump* or *slack* and sometimes *depression*. The common use today is *recession*, while the term *deflation* is kept to denote the measures the government takes to curb inflation.

75. J. Pen, *Modern Economics*, Penguin, London, 1958, p. 79.

76. If the promise to devalue is not kept, the public may lose faith in the government, but there is no harm in this.

77. "In a radical revision of his budget judgment of March 30 the Chancellor of the Exchequer listened rather more to City and industrial advice than to the economists whose forecasts of demand had gone badly astray. Faced with the paradox of high unemployment and continuing inflation, he came down in favour of a sharp deflationary stimulus that owes more to political judgment than to economic caution." (See column 1, "A Strong Boost to Consumer Demand," by David Wood, Political Editor.)

78. Lewis Coser, *The Functions of Social Conflict*, Routledge & Kegan Paul, London, 1956, pp. 121-22.

79. "Contradiction and conflict not only preceded unity but are oper-ative in it at every moment of its existence." (Georg Simmel, *Conflict*, tr. Kurt H. Wolff, The Free Press, Glencoe, Ill., 1955, p. 13.) "Conflict may indeed, from Utopian point of view, be conceived as one of the patterns contributing to the maintenance of the status quo." (Ralf Dahrendorf, *Class and Class Conflict in Industrial Society*, Routledge & Kegan Paul, London, 1959, p. 13.)

80. Lewis Coser, *The Functions of Social Conflict*, Routledge & Kegan Paul, London, 1956, p. 73.

81. See also Max Gluckman, *Custom and Conflict in Africa*, Blackwell, Oxford, 1955; John Rex, *Key Problems of Sociological Theory*, Rout-ledge & Kegan Paul, London, 1961, Chs. 7 and 8; Jessie Bernard "The Nature of Conflict," *International Sociological Association*, Paris, 1957, pp. 33-117.

82. Ralf Dahrendorf, *op. cit.*, p. 214.

83. *The Principles of Sociology*, Century, New York, n.d., pp. 164-65.

84. José Ortega y Gasset divides conflicts on a different basis: "Ques-tioning certain things but not questioning all, minor divergencies serve but to confirm and consolidate the underlying unanimity of the selective existence. But if dissent affects the basic layers of common belief on which the solidarity of the social body rests, then the State becomes a home divided, society dissociated, splitting up into two societies—that is, two groups with fundamentally divergent beliefs." (*Concord and Liberty*, Norton, New York, 1946, p. 15.) This, however, seems to be more the result of the split than its cause.

85. Frantz Fanon, *The Wretched of the Earth*, tr. Constance Farring-ton, Penguin, London, 1967, p. 73.

86. Lewis Coser, *op. cit.*, p. 118.

87. Livy, *The War with Hannibal*, tr. Aubrey de Selincourt, Penguin, London, 1965, p. 265.

88. "Chenu has very well described the evils that may result from a hasty and careless selection. He says: 'If the consequences of admitting men with weak constitutions into the army are bad in time of peace, they

are a great deal worse in time of war.'" S. Dumas and Vedel Peterson, *Losses of Life Caused by War*, Clarendon Press, Oxford, 1923, p. 104.

89. See *The Selective Service Regulations*, Department of State and Public Institutions, Washington, 1948. See also Conrad J. Lynn, *How to Stay Out of the Army*, M.R. Press, New York, 1%7.

90. "Since the officers have sometimes to lead him [the soldier] into greatest danger, he must be more afraid of his officers than of the dangers to which he is exposed." (J. F. C. Fuller, *Decisive Battles*, Eyre & Spottiswoode, London, 1939, p. 432.)

91. "People," said Thucydides, "grow angry when they suffer things that they are quite unused to suffer and when these things go on actually in front of their eyes." (*History of the Peloponnesian War*, tr. Rex Warner, Penguin, London, 1954, p. 103.)

92. Equipment for new recruits is distributed at random—the first in the queue gets the nearest package. If uniforms are issued at random, then the number of soldiers who can expect a perfect matched uniform is mathematically determined. If the expected number of perfect matches is E, the total number of soldiers is P, the number of different uniform sizes is n and p; is the number of people in the i-th group, then

$$E = \frac{1}{P}\sum_{i=1}^{n} p_i^2.$$

The expected proportion, e, of perfect matches will, therefore, be E/P.

We have, let us say, 40,000 people eligible for military service and the army has 40,000 uniforms for them in nine different sizes. Let us assume that the number of units in each size is as follows:

Size No.	No. of Uniforms
1	1,000
2	2,000
3	4,000
4	8,000
5	10,000
6	8,000
7	4,000
8	2,000
9	1,000

(The number of units of uniform in each given size is determined by the "normal" curve, the Gaussian equation for random distribution of sizes of people in any given population.)

According to the above formula, the expected number of perfect matches (if all the 40,000 are recruited) will be 6,500. That is, approximately 17 percent.

These calculations show that it is inevitable that some perfect matches will always turn up. However, it is still possible to modify the system of allocation so that the expected number of perfect matches is greatly reduced.

The allocation of a complete uniform to each recruit creates—as we have already seen—an expected number, E, of perfect matches. If the uniform is divided into two—one part, S_1, consisting of the top part (shirt) and the other part, S_2, the bottom part (trousers), and each part is issued independently at random, the expected proportion of perfect matches will be e^2. As e is smaller than 1, the expected proportion is greatly reduced. In our hypothetical army, if in the first instance we had an expected proportion, e, of $\dfrac{27}{160}$, then e^2 will be $\dfrac{729}{25,600}$. That is, an expected number of 1,139 (3 percent instead of 17 percent). If the uniform is further divided into coats, shoes, underwear and so forth, and each item is issued at random and independently of the other items, the expected number of perfect matches is further reduced:

$$e^3 = \frac{19{,}683}{4{,}096{,}000}; \; e^4 = \frac{531{,}421}{655{,}360{,}000} \cdots$$

$$e^n = \frac{27^n}{160^n}.$$

It can be seen that e^n tends to 0 as n tends to ∞.

93. In *My Reveries upon the Art of War*, Marshal de Saxe says: "The quality of food, water and kettles to make soup for a hundred men is more than would be sufficient for a thousand the way I propose, and the soup is never as good. Besides, the soldiers eat all sorts of unhealthy things such as pork and unripe fruit, which make them ill." (See T. R. Phillips, *Roots of Strategy*, Lane, London, 1943, p. 105.)

94. The history of cooking abounds with amateurs who have become supreme gastronomes: Brillat-Savarin, Grimond de Reynière, Rossini, Chateaubriand and many others.

95. Cecil Woodham-Smith, *The Reason Why*, Penguin, London, 1958, p. 177.

96. Ibid., p. 205.

97. Ronald Millar, *Kut: The Death of an Army*, Secker & Warburg, London, 1969, Appendix A and G.

98. "Bonaparte, who, on the day of a battle ate nothing until after it was over, had gone forward with his general staff and was a long way from his supply wagons. Seeing his enemies put to flight, he asked Dunand to prepare dinner for him. The master-chef at once sent men of the quartermaster's staff and ordnance corps in search of provisions. All they could find were three eggs, four tomatoes, six crayfish, a small hen, a little garlic, some oil and a saucepan. Using his bread ration, Dunand first made a *panade* with oil and water, and then, having drawn and jointed the chicken, browned it in oil and water, and fried the eggs in the same oil with a few cloves of garlic and the tomatoes. He poured over this mixture some water laced with brandy borrowed from the general's flask and put the crayfish on top to cook in the steam. The dish was served on a tin plate, the chicken surrounded by the fried eggs and crayfish, with the sauce poured over it. Bonaparte, after having feasted upon it, said to Dunand: 'You must feed me like this after every battle.'" (Prosper Mon-

tagné, *Larousse Gastronomique*, Hamlyn, London, 1961. Entry: "Marengo.")

99. It must be remembered that bad food is the result of bad provisions or of bad cooking or of both. Though bad cooking and bad provisions contribute equally to the badness of the dish, their contribution is not symmetrical: while bad provisions can be improved by good cooking, bad cooking cannot be improved by good provisions.

100. Xenophon admits in *The Persian Expedition* that "as far as I am concerned, I should certainly be happier with half the number of men if I were engaged in pursuit than I should be with twice the number on a retreat." (Tr. Rex Warner, Penguin, London, 1949, p. 236.)

101. Henri Jomini, *Summary of the Art of War,* ed. J. D. Hittle, Military Service Publishing Co., Hamburg, 1947, pp. 122-23.

102. *Ibid.*

103. Vegetius, in *The Military Institutions of the Romans*, devoted a special chapter to the subject: "Manner of Conducting a Retreat." Since then, the art of retreating has been largely neglected. In modern times it has been revived by the Russians who regard retreat as being worthy of serious consideration. In *How Russia Makes War* (Allen & Unwin, London, 1954, p. 161) Raymond L. Garthoff writes: "Retreat is a defensive form of manoeuvre and has been termed 'manoeuvre backward.'" Moreover, the Soviets have a special award, the Order of Kutuzov (created in 1942), awarded to high commanders exclusively for excellence in planned and controlled withdrawal, "This is the only award given by a state solely for retreat."

104. U.S. Army, *Drills and Ceremonies*, Department of the Army, FM 22-5, Washington, 1953, p. 1.

105. Marshal de Saxe had definite ideas about the role of legs in combat: "The foundation of training depends on the legs and not the arms. All the master of manoeuvres and combats is in the legs, and it is to the legs that we should apply ourselves. Whoever claims otherwise is but a fool and not only in the elements of what is called the profession of arms." (*Op. cit.*, p. 107.)

106. C. E. Callwell, *Small Wars*, H.M.S.O., London, 1906, p. 211.

THE WHITE FLAG PRINCIPLE

107. Karl von Clausewitz, *On War*, ed. Anatole Rapoport, Penguin, London, 1982, Bk. III, Ch. 8 ("Superiority of Numbers").

108. S. Dumas and Vedel Peterson, *op. cit.*, p. 40.

109. "Governments are interested in having people think the health condition of their armies perfect, and many of them lose no time in discharging soldiers who are taken seriously sick. Such unfortunates return home to die, their death being then charged to the mortality of the civil population and not to that of the army." *Ibid.*, p. 123.

110. Xenophon, *Memoirs of Socrates and the Symposium*, tr. Hugh Tredennick, Penguin, London, 1970, p. 242 (3, 4-7).

111. *A History of the Art of War*, Methuen, London, 1898, p. 163.

112. "The Army Act lays down that a man is guilty of cowardice when he displays 'an unsoldierly regard for his personal safety in the presence of the enemy' by shamefully deserting his post or laying down his arms." (Lord Moran, *The Anatomy of Courage*, Constable, London, 1945, p. 17.)

113. Shakespeare, *Antony and Cleopatra*, IV, xv, 86.

114. See Sir John Smyth, *The Victoria Cross*, Muller, London, 1965, p. 21

115. *Ibid.*, p. 51.

116. *Ibid.*, pp.29-30.

117. The London *Times*, 9 September 1969.

118. Suetonius mentions that Thermus awarded Julius Caesar the "civic crown of oak-leaves, at the storming of Mytilene, for saving a fellow soldier's life." (Suetonius, *The Twelve Caesars*, tr. Robert Graves, Penguin, London, 1957, p. 10.)

119. S. A. Stouffer et al., *The American Soldier*, Princeton University Press, Princeton, 1949, II, p. 124. The American attitude to the commander's place in the battle is the exact opposite of the ancient Romans' view. When Polybius discussed the best ways of employing troops, he said that the commander must lead the troops from behind: "What, I should like to know, can be less practical or more dangerous than a commander's being seen by all his troops, but seeing none of them?" (Polybius, *The Histories*, tr. W. R. Paton, Loeb Classical Library, Heinemann, London, 1925, X, 24.3.)

120. John Deane Potter, *A Soldier Must Hang*, New English Library, London, 1969, p. 128

121. *Ibid.*, p. 133.

122. Alfred Jarry, *Selected Works of Alfred Jarry*, ed. Roger Shattuck and Simon W. Taylor, Methuen, London, 1965, p. 125.

123. The Guardian, 18/07/2002, page 12

124. The *Daily Telegraph* reported on 4 June 1968: four colonels and two majors killed; the *Times* on 21 August: five Americans and two Australians; the *Times* on 21 September: fourteen Australians; the *Observer* on 16 November 1969: twenty-two killed and thirty-eight wounded; the *International Herald Tribune* on 24 November: one killed and thirty-three (including a battalion commander) wounded. The situation is very similar to that of the Second World War which produced—according to Asher Lee—"a shocking waste of bombing power and much needless killing of civilians because the targets attacked were the wrong ones." (*Air Power*, Duckworth, London, 1955, p. 19.)

125. The Guardian, 10/12/2001, p. 10.

126. Penguin, London, 1969, p. 28.

127. *Ibid.*, p.29.

128. *Encyclopaedia Britannica*.

129. The Guardian, 12/02/2002, p.9.

130. "Analysis of atomic damage in Nagasaki, Hiroshima and at the post-war atomic bomb trials at Bikini and New Mexico has shown that against certain resistant targets of concrete and steel, the atomic bomb can be less efficient than a series of rockets or armour-piercing bombs. In an attack on submarine pens heavily reinforced with concrete or on underground aircraft or other factories, the atomic bomb may be very wasteful. Modem steel and concrete cities will not suffer as Hiroshima and Nagasaki did. . . . To use atomic bombs against airfield targets would be like using heavy artillery to shoot rabbits. It is not only uneconomical, but you are unlikely to have enough shells to kill most of the rabbits." (Asher Lee, *op. cit.*, p. 22.)

131. See also article in The *Sunday Times* on 8 February 1970: "The Most Dangerous Tombs in the World."

132. The Guardian, 28/12/2001, p. 1, see also p. 6.

133. The Guardian, 01/03/2002, p. 16

134. Lt. Burne says: "Luck, though it is no doubt true that luck in the long run pans out evenly, this is not true of a short campaign, still less of a battle. It can, in fact, play a disconcertingly prominent part in the issue." (Alfred H. Burne, *The Art of War on Land*, Methuen, London, 1944, p. 5.)

135. A line of communication, or LOC in short, is the "line or lines that connect the army with its base" (Alfred H. Burne, *The Art of War on Land*, Methuen, London, 1944, p. 24.) The base (the base of operations) is "the portion of the country from which it starts when it takes the offensive, to which it retreats when necessary, and by which it is supported when it takes position to cover the country defensively." (Henri Jomini, *Summary of the Art of War*, ed. J. D. Hittle, Military Service Publishing Co., Harrisburg, Pa., 1947.)

136. *The Second World War*, Eyre & Spottiswoode, London, 1948, p. 186.

137. The real value of flight for the enemy's victory has divided the military into two camps ever since. Vegetius in *The Military Institutions of the Romans* (A.D. 378) discusses it: "Generals unskilled in war think a victory incomplete unless the enemy are so straitened in their ground or so entirely surrounded by numbers as to have no possibility of escape . . . the maxim of Scipio, that a golden bridge should be made for a flying enemy, has been much commended." (Tr. John Clarke; see T. R. Phillips, *Roots of Strategy*, Lane, London, 1943, p. 87.)

138. In this sense we can rightly say that a guerilla army is always suffering defeat. But as its line of communication is so short as to be virtually nonexistent, the value of the defeats it sustains is almost nil.

139. "Von Clausewitz and the great military writer Colonel Henderson consider pursuit to be a principle. It is an accepted military maxim that 'touch once gained should never be lost,' and this is especially applicable to the pursuit. To gain the full fruits of victory the pursuit must be vigorous and sustained." (Alfred H. Burne, *op. cit.*, p. 22.) See also footnote 3 on page 86.

140. Karl von Clausewitz, *On War*, quoted in J. F. C. Fuller, *The Conduct of War*, Eyre & Spottiswoode, London, 1962, p. 72.

141. Theodore Lyman, *Meade's Headquarters, 1863–1865*, ed. G.R. Agassiz, Massachusetts Historical Society, Boston, 1922, p. 224. See also J. F. C. Fuller, *The Second World War*, Eyre & Spottiswoode, London, 1948, p. 42: "... fire power in the defence is defence is more destructive than fire power in the attack."

142. *Correspondance inedited de Napoleon 1er, conservée aux Archives de la Guerre*, ed. Ernest Picard and Louis Tuetey, Paris, 1912, XIII, No. 10558; tr. L.S. Houghton, Duffield, New York, 1913.

143. The Persian army numbered, according to some authorities, as many as 1,000,000 men, as against 47,000 of Alexander's.

144. The analysis of the battle is based on Sir Edward Creasy's *The Fifteen Decisive Battles of the World*, Macmillan, London, 1901; Major General Fuller's *Decisive Battles*, Eyre & Spottiswoode, London, 1939, and *The Generalship of Alexander the Great*, Eyre & Spottiswoode, London, 1958; Alfred H. Burne, *op. cit.*; and Arrian, *The Campaigns of Alexander*, tr. Aubrey de Selincourt, Penguin, London, 1971.

145. New, revolutionary weapons require new tactics and new strategies only in the narrow, technical sense. When it comes to basic, fundamental principles, like the ones we are discussing in this chapter, warfare has not changed since ancient times. It is so recognized by all. This is why modern military textbooks abound in examples from classical battles. Major General Fuller, in his book about the Second World War, illustrated modern strategical and tactical problems with ancient examples, saying: "On first thoughts it may seem that the introduction of aircraft introduced a new form of attack and defence—namely the vertical. But this is not so. In its day the Roman testudo was as important a means of defence against vertically falling projectiles as anti-aircraft fire and concrete shelters are now. And when at the battle of Hastings, on 14 October 1066, William the Conqueror ordered his archers to fire their arrows into the sky so that they would fall vertically on Harold's army, in an elementary way he was doing nothing more than what bombing aircraft now do, and frequently with less decisive effect. From this brief excu-

sion into the past it will be seen, though the means of attack and defence have changed out of all recognition, the forms of attack and defence remain constant." (*The Second World War*, p. 46.)

146. B. H. Liddell Hart, *Strategy: The Indirect Approach*, Faber & Faber, London, 1967 ed., pp. 297-98.

147. *Ibid.*, p.324

148. "The whole French army disintegrated, in a '*sauve qui peut*,' and the Allied army was launched into the most implacable pursuit of the eighteenth century. Marlborough did not himself halt till he was over twelve miles from the battlefield, having been nineteen hours in the saddle. Even then his rest was only for two hours. At 2 AM he was in the saddle again, and driving on the pursuit. The English horse and foot drove on right through the night, and the cavalry did not draw rein till within sight of Louvain, over twenty miles from the battlefield. Five thousand unwounded prisoners and every single French gun were taken; the French army had ceased to exist." (Alfred H. Burne, *op. cit.*, pp. 144-5.)

149. See Sir Winston Churchill, *The Second World War*, Cassell, London, 1951, Bk. 1, Chs. 4, 5.

150. For a full account of the battle see J. F. C. Fuller, *Decisive Battles* and Alfred H. Burne, *op. cit.*

151. See Livy, *The War with Hannibal*, tr. Aubrey de Selincourt, Penguin, London, 1965, pp. 144-50. Also Polybius, *The Histories*, tr. W. R. Paton, Loeb Classical Library, Heinemann, London, 1925.

152. J. F. C. Fuller, *The Second World War*, p. 44.

153. The damage suffered by the community as a result of war is usually exaggerated. In *Statistics of Deadly Quarrels* (Atlantic Books, Stevens, London, 1960, p. 152), Lewis F. Richardson calculated the total number of people killed in 126 years, from 1820 to 1945, and compared it with the number of people that have died during the same period of any other causes. While all deaths amounted to 3,800,000,000 men, the total of deaths from deadly quarrels was only 58,400,000. That is, a mere 1.6 percent.

154. Herbert C. Fooks, *Prisoners of War*, Stowell, Federalsburg, 1924, pp. 114-15.

155. Jerry Rose and Grant Wolfkill, *Reported to be Alive*, Simon & Schuster, New York, 1965, p. 29.

156. Allen & Unwin, London, 1962, p. 58.

157. Before the white flag had become the symbol of surrender, it was used as a symbol of sovereignty. The white flag is known to have been the flag of the Emperor Chou in China, in 1122 B.C.; the standard of Genghis Khan; the flag of the Banu Umayyad dynasty in the seventh century and the banner of Baldwin, among many others. In *Flags of All Nations*, published in Amsterdam around 1865, the white flag is mentioned as being still in use as a naval ensign in Portugal, Netherlands, Brazil and Spain. As a token of surrender, the white flag is first mentioned by Tacitus: "Headed by white flags and tokens of surrender they [the people of Vienne] went out to meet the troops. . . ." (*Histories*, tr. Kenneth Wellesley, Penguin, London, 1964, Bk. 1, 66.)

158. Bernal Diaz, *The Conquest of New Spain*, Penguin, London, 1963, pp. 35-36.

159. E. M. C. Barraclough, *Flags of the World*, Warne, London, 1969, p. 8.

160. *Ibid.*, p. 9.

161. "Winter is so unfavourable to the carrying on of military operations that in ancient times and during the Middle Ages almost the only campaigns known, so to speak, were conducted in the summer." S. Dumas and Vedel Peterson, *Losses of Life Caused by War*, Clarendon Press, Oxford, 1923, p. 81.

162. During the First World War it was reported that the signals of surrender were "abused by the Germans by carrying a small pistol sarcastically called the 'Kamerad' pistol in the hand and firing with it after indicating a desire to surrender." Another story tells about a captured German officer who shot an American [Lieutenant Haycock] with a small pistol concealed in his fists. (see Herbert C. Fooks, *op. cit.*, pp. 115, 117.)

163. "This arises under the convention which provides that all that is captured in war becomes legally the property of the captors." (Polybius, *The Histories*, tr. W. R. Paton, Loeb Classical Library, Heinemann, London, 1925, Bk. I, p. 35.)

164. William Slim, *Unofficial History*, Corgi Books, London, 1970, p. 50.

165. It was rumoured at the time that someone from the Iraqi Embassy bought a copy of *The White Flag Principle* when it was first published in London in 1972 by Alan Lane (Penguin Press).

166. This is based on the assumption that your intelligence services are up to date.

167. International law states: "As soon as possible after the capture, prisoners are removed from the danger zone. . . . The internment camps must be outside the combat zone. . . . Shelters against the hazards of war and aerial bombardment must be provided and prisoners must be permitted to use them." (L. Oppenheim, *International Law*, Longmans, London, 1952 [7th ed.], II, 378 [par. 127, 127a]. See also Herbert C. Fooks, *Prisoners of War*, Stowell, Federalsburg, Md., 1924, p. 137.)

168. The obligation of the captor to provide all of the captive's necessities is clearly defined: "The conditions under which the prisoners are interned must be as favourable as those of the troops of the Detaining Power quartered in that area. This applies especially to the size of dormitories and to the provisions of bedding and blankets. The Detaining Power must ensure that prisoners are and remain properly clothed. . . . Sufficient food, taking account of the habitual diet of the prisoners, must be provided to maintain good health and prevent loss of weight or the development of nutritional deficiencies." (Oppenheim, *op. cit.*, pp. 379-80.) Sports facilities for POWs have been provided for by many international conventions: Stockholm in 1916; Copenhagen in 1917; and the American-German convention of 1918. Recreation rooms have become obligatory since the Anglo-German convention of 1918 and the American-German convention of the same year. The organization of schools, libraries and the presentation of theatrical and similar entertainment in prison camps has been stipulated in Copenhagen, in the American-German convention and in Stockholm.

169. "It is a fundamental principle that prisoners must at all times be humanely treated. . . . Prisoners of war may not, for example, be made the subject of physical mutilation or medial and scientific experiment.

Likewise, they must be protected from the curiosity, violence, intimidation and insult of the local population." Ibid., pp. 376-77 (par. 126b).

170. *A Kut Prisoner*, Lane, London, 1920, p. 36.

171. Oppenheim, *op. cit.*, p. 385.

172. "Prisoners are permitted to make complaints about the conditions of their captivity; even if such complaints are unfounded, they must not give rise to punishment." *Ibid.*, p. 386.

173. To appreciate life in captivity, one must compare it with the lot of the fighting soldier. While German soldiers in the Second World War complained bitterly about their conditions in Russian captivity, few have said a word about their lot before they were captured. However, some information has been revealed. Following is what a German soldier wrote: "This is what had been happening with the soldiers of the Sixth Army. From September onward the fighting men of many divisions had received not much more than 1,800 calories a day, and they had long become familiar with hunger. About one third of them had survived jaundice or intestinal troubles in the autumn, many of them had contracted typhus or malaria in the river Don. From the end of November onwards they had been housed in fox-holes on the bare steppe, under conditions of snow, ice and damp; their food had consisted of four ounces of bread and the meagre flesh of nags which had starved to death. Winter clothing had grown more and more scarce. At one regimental gun position we had seen a soldier's store of woollen socks: a single pair, and they were more holes and shreds of wool than socks." (Hans Dibold, *Doctor of Stalingrad*, tr. H. C. Stevens, Hutchinson, London, 1958, pp. 27-28.)

174. Arthur Ponsonby, *Falsehood in Wartime*, Allen & Unwin, London, 1928, p. 22.

175. "In order to stimulate the patriotism of the people, to create the proper atmosphere towards the enemy, it is considered essential to attribute to him the faults of heartless cruelty, a lack of all human principles, and to lay at his door the impossible of all crimes, including rape, massacre and murder. . . . Tales of the heartless and ruthless murder of the wounded prisoners, of deliberate starvation, the lack of care, etc., early found their way into newspapers of all the nations at war." Daniel J.

McCarthy, *The Prisoner of War in Germany*, Moffat & Yard, New York, 1918, pp. 1-2. See also J. F. C. Fuller, *The Conduct of War*, Eyre & Spottiswoode, London, 1962, p. 179.

176. "The military prisoner, who loses his liberty in the stress of battle, finds in captivity a rest from his toil, and in the calm feels at first a true relief." (A.L. Vischer, *Barbed Wire Disease*, tr. S.A. Kinnier Wilson, Bale, London, 1919, p. 46)

177. *Hell in Siberia*, tr. Eleanor Brockett, Hall, London, 1957, p. 12

178. Ssu-ma Ch'ien, *Shi Ji* (Records of the Grand Historian), 111: *The Biographies of General Wei Ch'ing and the Swift Cavalry General Ho Ch'u-ping*, tr. Burton Watson, Columbia University Press, New York and London, 1961, p. 204.

179. *Ibid.*, p. 86 (*Shih Ji* 30: *The Balanced Standard*). See also p. 84: "Generous gifts were also given to the tens of thousands of enemy captives, and food and clothing were supplied to them by the district officials."

180. Marcus Tullius Cicero, *De Officiis*, tr. G.B. Gardiner, Methuen, London, 1899, I, 11.

181. *The Decline and Fall of the Roman Empire*, Chatto & Windus, London, 1960 ed., pp. 100-101.

182. *Ibid.*, p. 119.

183. Alden J. Mason, *The Ancient Civilizations of Peru*, Penguin, London, 1969, p. 82.

184. *The Law of Nations*, tr. Joseph Chitty, Sweet, Stevens & Maxwell, London, 1834, p. 354.

185. "My whole impression of the camp authorities at Wittenberg was utterly unlike that which I received in every other camp I visited in Germany. Instead of regarding their charges as honourable prisoners of war, it appeared to me the men were regarded as criminals." *G.B. Parliamentary Papers 1916*, Cd. 8235, p. 4.

186. Ronald Millar, *Kut: The Death of an Army*, Secker & Warburg, London, 1969, p. 1.

187. *A Kut Prisoner*, Lane, London, 1920, pp. 34-35, 37-40, 56, 82.

188. *Besieged in Kut and After*, Blackwood, London, 1917, p. 295

189. *Return Ticket*, Collins, London, 1968, pp. 61-62.

190. Sydney Smith, *Wing's Day*, Collins, London, 1968, pp. 61-62.

191. *The Colditz Story and the Later Days*, Hodder & Stoughton, London, 1962, p. 93.

192. *Ibid.*, p. 94.

193. Eugene Kinkhead, *Why They Collaborated*, Longmans, London, 1960, p. 106.

194. Vischer, *op. cit.*, pp. 67, 70-71.

195. *Ibid.*, p. 50. See also W. Hellpach, *Nervenleben und Weltanschanung*, W. Engelmann, Wiesbaden, 1906; R. Bing, "*Uber den Begriff der Neurastherie*," *Klinik medizin.*, No. 5, 1908; W. V. Bechterev, *Die Bedeutung der Suggestion im Sozialen Leben*, Tract 39 of the collection *Grenzfragen des Nerven und Seelenlebens*, 1908.

196. See L. Huot and P. Voivenel, *Le Cafard*, Grasset, Paris, 1918.

197. Vischer, *op. cit.*, pp. 51-52.

198. *Ibid.*, p. 57.

199. "*Cet état d'inactivité et de reclusion, joint aux effêts du climat et au manqué de société et de distractions, devait necessairement occasionner des maladies à un homme don't les facultés morales et physiques avaient, depuis sa grande jeunesse, été employees de la manière la plus active.*" From the diary of Napoleon's physician, Dr. Barry E. O'Meara, *Recueil de pieces authentiques sur le captif de St. Hélène*, Paris, 1822.

200. "The attempt has already been made to base certain types of psychoneurosis on social and historical conditions. The American physician, Beard, who introduced to medicine the conception of neurasthenia, described the neurasthenic symptoms complex as the disease of the American businessman; he emphasized the fact that neurasthenia could develop only in the soil afforded by American commercialism." Vischer, *op. cit.*, p. 58.

201. "I can think of no sport that is the peer of escape, where freedom, life and loved ones are the prize of victory, and death the possible though by no means inevitable price of failure." Reid, *op. cit.*, Prologue.

202. Kinkhead, *op. cit.*, p. 109.

203. Burton C. Andrus, *The Infamous of Nuremberg*, Frewin, London, 1969, p. 30.

204. *Ibid.*, p.38.
205. The Guardian, 26/07/02, page 2
206. *Op. cit.*, pp. 42-43.

Bibliography

Aeneas Tacticus, *Military Manual*, tr. Illinois Greek Club, Loeb Classical
  Library, Heinemann, London, 1923.
——, *On Siegecraft*, ed. W. Hunter, Oxford, 1822.
Andrus, Burton C., *The Infamous of Nuremberg*, Frewin, London 1969.
Archilochus, *The Penguin Book of Greek Verse*, ed. C. Trypanis, London,
  1971.
Arendt, Hannah, "Reflections on Violence," *The New York Review of
  Books*, 29 Feb. 1969.
Ariga, Nagao, *La guerre Russo-Japonaise*, Pedune, Paris, 1907.
Aristotle, *Politics*, tr. T. A. Sinclair, Penguin, London, 1962.
Arrian, *The Campaigns of Alexander*, tr. Aubrey de Sélincourt, Penguin,
  London, 1971.
Asclepiodotus, tr. Illinois Greek Club, Loeb Classical Library, Heine-
  mann, London, 1923.
Attwill, Ken, *The Rising Sunset*, Hale, London, 1957.
Ayres, L. P., *The War with Germany*, Government Printing Office, Wash-
  ington, 1919.

Bain, Joe S., *Pricing, Distribution and Employment*, Holt, New York, 1949.

Barber, Charles H., *Besieged in Kut and After*, Blackwood London, 1917.

Barnett, Correlli, *The Swordbearers*, Eyre & Spottiswoode, London, 1963.

Barraclough, E. M. C., *Flags of the World*, Warne, London, 1969.

Beafre, André, *An Introduction to Strategy*, tr. R. H. Barry, Faber & Faber, London, 1965.

Bechterev, W. V., *Die Bedeutung der Suggestion im Sozialen Leben*, Tract 39 of the collection *Grenzfragen des Nerven md Seelenlebens*, 1908.

Bernard, Jessie, *The Nature of Conflict*, International Sociological Association, Paris, 1957, pp. 33-117.

Bing, R., *Über den Begriff der Neurastherie*, *Klinik medizin.*, No. 5, Berlin and Vienna, 1908.

Bishop, H. C. W., *A Kut Prisoner*, Lane, London, 1920.

Bodart, Gaston, *Losses of Life in Modern War*, Clarendon Press, Oxford, 1916.

Boulding, Kenneth E., *Economic Analysis*, Harper, New York, 1941.

Brickhill, Paul, *The Great Escape*, Faber & Faber, London, 1966.

Brillat-Savarin, Anthelme, *The Philosopher in the Kitchen*, tr. Anne Drayton, Penguin, London, 1970.

Burne, Alfred H., *The Art of War on Land*, Methuen, London, 1944.

Bulow, J. C., *Japan's Decision to Surrender*, Stanford University Press, Stanford, 1954.

Caesar, Julius, *The Civil War*, Penguin, London, 1967.

Callwell, C. E., *Small Wars*, H.M.S.O., London, 1906.

Cambridge Medieval History, ed. J. R. Tanner et al., Cambridge University Press, Cambridge, 1957.

Cartwright, H. A., and Harrison, M. C. C., *Within Four Walls*, Arnold, London, 1930.

Catton, Bruce, *The Penguin Book of the American Civil War*, London, 1966. (American ed.: *American Heritage Picture History of the Civil War*, Doubleday, New York, 1960.)

Chamberlain, Basil Hall, *Things Japanese* (1890), Kegan Paul, London, 1939.

Chapman, Spenser F., *The Jungle Is Neutral*, Chatto & Windus, London, 1963.

Churchill, Sir Winston, *The Second World War*, Cassell, London, 1951.

Cicero, *De Officiis*, tr. George B. Gardiner, Methuen, London, 1899.

———, *Selected Political Speeches*, tr. Michael Grant, Penguin, London, 1969.

Clarke, Robin, *We All Fall Down*, Penguin, London, 1969.

Clausewitz, Karl von, *On War*, ed. Anatol Rapoport, Penguin, London, 1968.

Collier, Basil, *The War in the Far East*, Heinemann, London, 1969.

Collis, Louise, *Soldier in Paradise*, Joseph, London, 1965.

Coser, Lewis, *The Functions of Social Conflict*, Routledge & Kegan Paul, London, 1956.

Crawford, Hew T. M., *The Long Green Tunnel*, Joseph, London, 1967.

Creasy, Sir Edward, *The Fifteen Decisive Battles of the World*, Macmillan, London, 1901.

Cuddon, Eric (ed.), *War Crimes Trials*, Hodge, London, 1952.

Curtius Quintus, tr. John C. Rolfe, Loeb Classical Library, Heinemann, London, 1946.

Dahrendorf, Ralf, *Class and Class Conflict in Industrial Society*, Routledge & Kegan Paul, London, 1959.

Damon, Albert, Stoudt, Howard W., and McFarland, Ross A., *The Human Body in Equipment Design*, Harvard University Press, Cambridge, 1966.

Davidson, Eugene, *The Trial of the Germans*, Macmillan, New York, 1966.

Deane-Drummond, Anthony, *Return Ticket*, Collins, London,1967.

Díaz, Bernal, *The Conquest of New Spain*, Penguin, London, 1963.

Dibold, Hans, *Doctor at Stalingrad*, tr. H.C. Stevens, Hutchinson, London, 1958.

Dickinson, John, *The Writings of*, ed. Paul Leicester-Ford, The Historical Society of Pennsylvania, Philadelphia, 1895.

Diodorus the Sicilian, *The Historical Library of*, tr. G. Booth, London, 1814.

Dumas, S., and Peterson, Vedel, *Losses of Life Caused by War*, Clarendon Press, Oxford, 1923.

Edwards, T. J., *Standards, Guidons and Colours of the Commonwealth Forces*, Gale & Polden, Aldershot, 1953.

Elstop, Peter, *Spanish Prisoner*, Macmillan, London, 1939.

Evans, A. J., *The Escaping Club*, Panther, London, 1957.

Fall, Bernard B., *Street Without Joy*, Pall Mall Press, London, 1964.

Fanon, Frantz, *The Wretched of the Earth*, tr. Constance Farrington, Penguin, London, 1967.

Feis, Herbert, *Japan Subdued*, Princeton University Press, Princeton, 1961.

First Conference of German Prisoners of War Privates and Non-Commissioned Officers in the Soviet Union, Foreign Languages Publishing House, Moscow, 1941.

Fiscal Policy of a Balanced Economy, Organisation for Economic Cooperation and Development, Paris, Dec. 1968.

Flags of All Nations, Weytingh & Brave, Amsterdam, 1868-70.

Flory, William E. S., *Prisoners of War*, American Council of Public Affairs, Washington, 1942.

Foch, Ferdinand, *The Principles of War*, tr. Hilaire Belloc, Chapman & Hall, London, 1918.

Fooks, Herbert C., *Prisoners of War*, Stowell, Federalsburg , 1924.

Frederick the Great, *Military Instructions for the Generals*; see T. R. Phillips, *Roots of Strategy*.

Fuller, J. F. C., *The Conduct of War*, Eyre & Spottiswoode, London, 1962.

——, *Decisive Battles*, Eyre & Spottiswoode, London, 1939.

——, *The Generalship of Alexander the Great*, Eyre & Spottiswoode, London, 1958.

——, *The Second World War*, Eyre & Spottiswoode, London, 1948.

Galbraith, J. K., *The Affluent Society*, Hamilton, London, 1958. (American ed.: Houghton Mifflin, Boston, 1958.)

——, *The Great Crash, 1929*, Penguin, London, 1955. (American ed.: Houghton Mifflin, Huston, 1955.)

Garthoff, Raymond L., *How Russia Makes War*, Allen & Unwin, London, 1954.

George, Henry, *Progress and Poverty*, Robert Shalkenbach Foundation, New York, 1933.

Gibbon, Edward, *The Decline and Fall of the Roman Empire*, Chatto & Windus, London, 1960.

Glaser, Barney G., and Strauss, Anslem L., *Awareness of Dying*, Weidenfeld & Nicholson, London, 1966.

Glover, T. R., *The Ancient World*, Penguin, London, 1944.

Gluckman, Max, *Custom and Conflict in Africa*, Blackwell, Oxford, 1955.

Goldoni, Carlo, *Memoirs of*, tr. John Black, Colburn, London, 1814.

Greek Political Oratory, tr. A. N. W. Saunders, Penguin, London, 1970.

Greene, T.N. (ed.), *The Guerilla and How to Fight Him*, Praeger, New York, 1962.

Guevara, Che, *Guerrilla Warfare*, Penguin, London, 1969.

Hargest, J., *Experience in Captivity*, Empire Parliament Association, Londun, 1944.

Harrison, Kenneth, *The Brave Japanese*, Angus & Robertsun, London, 1967.

Harrison, M. C. C., and Cartwright, H. A., *Within Four Walls*, Arnold, London, 1930.

Harvey, Frank, *Air War: Vietnam*, Bantam, New York, 1961.

Hasek, Jaruslav, *The Good Soldier Schweik*, tr. P. Selver, Penguin, Lundun, 1951.

Heller, Joseph, *Catch-22*, Simon & Schuster, New York, l96l.

Hellpach, W., *Nervenleben und Weltanschauung*, W. Engelmann, Wiesbaden, 1906.

Herodian, *Histories*, tr. C. R. Whiuacker, Loeb Classical Library, Heinemann, London, 1969.

Hitler, Adolf, *The Testament of Adolf Hitler* (The Hitler-Bormann Documents, Feb.-Apr., 1945), tr. R. H. Stevens, Cassell, London, 1959.

Hobbes, Thomas, *Leviathan* (1651), Dent, London, 1914.

Holls, Frederick W., *The Peace Conference of the Hague*, Macmillan, London, n.d.

Homer, *The Iliad*, tr. E.V. Rieu, Penguin, London, 1969.

Horace, *Epistles*, ed. D. A. W. Dilke, Methuen, London, 1854.

Howard, Michael (ed.), *The Theory and Practice of War*, Cassell, London, 1965.

Hulme, F. E., *Flags of the World*, Warne, New York, 1897.

Hulton, Bernard J., *School of Spies*, Spearman, London, 1961.

Huot, L., and Voivenel, P., *Le Cafard*, Grasset, Paris, 1918.

Hythe Musketry Course, Gale & Pulden, Aldershot, 1914.

Ibn Jubayr, *Travells* (1183), tr. R. J. C. Broadhurst, Cape, London, 1952.

Jackson, Robert, *A Taste of Freedom*, Baker, London, 1964.

Jarry, Alfred, *Selected Works of*, ed. Roger Shattuck and Simon W. Taylor, Methuen, London, 1965.

Joesten, Joachim, *They Call It Intelligence: Spies and Spy Techniques Since World War II*, Abelard-Schuman, New York, 1963.

Joinville, Sire de, *Saint Louis, King of France*, tr. James Hutton, Sampson, London, 1892.

Jomini, Henri, *Summary of the Art of War*, ed. J. D. Hittle, Military Service Publishing Co., Harrisburg, 1947.

Jones, E.H., *The Road to En-Dor*, Lane, London, 1920.

Jordanes, *The Gothic History*, tr. C. C. Mierow, Oxford University Press, London, 1915.

Josephus, Flavius, *The Jewish War*, tr. G. A. Williamson, Penguin, London, 1967.

Kahn, Herman, *Thinking About the Unthinkable*, Weidenfeld & Nicolson, London, 1962.

Keesing's Contemporary Archives. (American ed.: Horizon Press, New York, 1962.)

Kendal, Burt, and Leasor, James, *The One that Got Away*, Collins & Joseph, London, 1956.

Keynes, John Maynard, *The General Theory of Employment*, Interest and Money, Macmillan, London, 1967.

Kingston-McCloughry, E. J., *The Spectrum of Strategy*, Cape, London, 1964.

Kinkhead, Eugene, *Why They Collaborated*, Longman, London, 1960.

Knowles, Christine, *A Small Book of Comfort for Those in Captivity*, Muller, London, 1941.

Lao-tzu, *Tao tê Ching*, tr. D. C. Lau, Penguin, London, 1963.

Lawson, Don, The War of 1812, Abelard-Schuman, New York, 1916.

Layman, Theodore, *Meade Headquarter*, ed. G. R. Agassiz, Massachusetts Historical Society, Boston, 1922.

Lee, Asher, *Air Power*, Duckworth, London, 1955.

Lerner, A. P., "Functional Finance and the Federal Debt," *Social Research*, New York, 1943.

Lewin, L. C., Report from Iron Mountain, Penguin, London, 1967. (American ed.: Dell Publishing Co., Inc., New York, 1969.)

Lewis, Michael, *Napoleon and His British Captives*, Allen & Unwin, London, 1962.

Liddell Hart, B. H., *Strategy: The Indirect Approach*, Faber & Faber, London, 1967 ed.

Livy, *The War with Hannibal* (Bks. XXI-XXX of the *History of Rome from its Foundation*), tr. Aubrey de Selincourt, Penguin, London, 1965.

Lloyd and Tempelhoff, *The History of the Seven Years' War in Germany*, tr. C. N. Smith, War Office, London, 1808.

Locke, John, *A Letter to a Friend Concerning Usury*, London, 1621.

Luttwak, Edward, *Coup d'État*, Allen Lane The Penguin Press, London, 1968.

Lynn, Conrad J., *How to Stay Out of the Army*, M.R. Press, New York, 1967.

McCarthy, Daniel J., *The Prisoner of War in Germany*, Moffat & Yard, New York, 1918.

Machiavelli, Niccoló, *The Prince*, tr. Luigi Ricci, Mentor, London, 1952.

Macgeorge, A., Flags: *Some Accounts of Their History and Uses*, Blackie, London, 1881.

Mackintosh, J. M., *War and the Doctor*, Oliver & Boyd, London, 1940.

Macpherson, W. G., *Medical Services General History*, H.M.S.O., London, 1921.

Malaparte, Curzio, *Coup d'État: The Technique of the Revolution*, E.P. Dutton, New York, 1932.

Malthus, Thomas, *An Essay on the Principle of Population* (1798), Penguin, London, 1970.

Mandeville, Bernard, *The Fable of the Bees* (1723). Penguin, London, 1970.

Mao Tse-tung, *Quotations*, Foreign Languages Press, Peking, 1967.

Mao Tse-tung, *Strategic Problems of China's Revolutionary War*, Foreign Languages Press, Peking, 1954.

Marriot, J. A. R., *The Eastern Question*, Clarendon Press, Oxford, 1918.

Marshal, Alfred, *The Principles of Economics*, Macmillan, London, 1890.

Mason, Alden J., *The Ancient Civilizations of Peru*, Penguin, London, 1969.

Mayer, Kurt B., *Class and Society*, Random House, New York, 1966.

Michailowsky-Danielewsky and Miliutin, *Geschichte des Krieges Russlands mit Frankreich unter der Regierturg Kaiser Pauls I im Jahre 1799*, tr. C. Schmitt, Vol. 1, Munich, 1856, p. 2.

Millar, Ronald, *Kut: The Death of an Army*, Secker & Warburg, London, 1969.

Ministry of Defence, *Drill*, H.M.S.O., London, 1965.

Mitford, A. B., *Tales of Old Japan*, Macmillan, London, 1890.

Montagné, Prosper, *Larousse Gastronomique*, Hamlyn, London, 1961.

Montgomery of Alamein, *A History of Warfare*, Collins, London, 1968.

Montgomery, John D., *Forced to Be Free*, University of Chicago Press, Chicago, 1957.

Montross, Lynn, *War Through the Ages*, Harper & Row, New York, 1960.

Moran, Lord, *The Anatomy of Courage*, Constable, London, 1945.

Morgenstern, Oskar, and von Neuman, John, *Theory of Games and Economic Behavior*, Princeton University Press, Princeton, 1947.

Mumford, Lewis, *Technics and Civilization*, Routledge, London, 1934.

Napoleon Bonaparte, Correspondence of Napoléon 1er, Publiée Par Ordre de l'Empereur Napoléon III, Paris, 1858-1859.

——, Unpublished Correspondence of Napoleon I, preserved in the War Archives. ed. Ernest Picard and Louis Tuetey, tr. Louise Seymour Houghton, Duffield, New York, 1913.

New American Encyclopedia, Publishers' Company, Washington, 1963.

Nicolson, Harold, *Diplomacy*, Oxford University Press, New York, 1964.

Nork, Karl, *Hell in Siberia*, tr. Eleanor Brockett, Hall, London, 1957.

Oman, Charles, *A History of the Art of War*, Methuen, London, 1898.

O'Meara, Barry E., *Recueil de pièces authentiques sur le captif de St. Hélène*, Paris, 1822.

Onasander, tr. Illinois Greek Club, Loeb Classical Library, Heinemann, London, 1923.

Oppenheim, L., International Law (7th ed.), Longmans, London, 1952.

Ortega y Gasset, José, *Concord and Liberty*, Norton, New York, 1946.

Pacific War Research Society, *Japan's Longest Day*, Corgi Books, London, 1969.

Parkins, Ray, *The Sword and the Blossom*, Hogarth, London, 1968.

Peers, William R., and Brelis, Dean, *Behind the Burma Road*, Hale, London, 1963.

Pen, J., *Modern Economics*, Penguin, London, 1958.

Pernoud, Régine, *The Crusaders*, Secker & Warburg, London, 1960.

Perrin, W. G., *British Flags*, Cambridge University Press, Cambridge, 1922.

Philips, E. D., *The Mongols*, Thames & Hudson, London, 1969.

Phillips, T. R., *Roots of Strategy*, Lane, London, 1943.

Plato, The Republic, tr. H. D. P. Lee, Penguin, London, 1955.

Plutarch, *The Rise and Fall of Athens*, tr. Ian Scott-Kilvert, Penguin, London, 1960.

Polybius, *The Histories*, tr. W. R, Paton, Loeb Classical Library, Heinemann, London, 1925.

Ponsonby, Arthur, *Falsehood in War Time*, Allen & Unwin, London, 1928.

Potter, John Deane, *A Soldier Must Hang*, New English Library, London, 1969.

Prescott, W. H., *Conquest of Mexico*, Dent, New York, 1909.

Prescott, W. H., *History of the Conquest of Peru*, Dent, New York, 1908.

Procopius, *The Secret History*, tr. G. A. Williamson, Penguin, London, 1966.

The Queen's Regulations and Orders for the Army, Parker, Furnival & Parker, London, 1844.

Rapoport, Amos, and Watson, Newton, "Cultural Variability in Physical Standards", *Transactions of the Bartlett Society*, Vol. VI, London, 1968.

Reich, Emil, *Selected Documents*, King, London, 1905.

Rapoport, Anatol, "The Use and Misuse of Game Theory", Scientific American, Vol. 207, No. 6, New York, 1962.

Reid, P. R., *The Colditz Story and the Later Days*, Hodder & Stoughton, London, 1962.

Rex, John, *Key Problems of Sociological Theory*, Routledge & Kegan Paul, London, 1961.

Ricardo, David, *Principles of Political Economy*, 6th ed., Penguin, London, 1971.

Richardson, Lewis F., *Statistics of Deadly Quarrels*, Atlantic Books, Stevens, London, 1960.

Ross, E. Alsworth, *The Principles of Sociology*, Century, New York, 1920.

Russell of Liverpool, Lord, *The Knights of Bushido*, Cassell, London, 1958.

Sallust, *The Jugurthine War* and *The Conspiracy of Cataline*, tr. S. A. Handford, Penguin, London, 1963.

Salter, Sir Arthur, *Recovery - The Second Effort*, Bell, London, 1934.

Saxe, Maurice de, *My Reveries upon the Art of War*; see T. R. Phillips, *Roots of Strategy*.

Seth, Ronald, *Caporeto*, Macdonald, London, 1965.

Shakespeare, *Antony and Cleopatra*.

Sierksma, K. L., *Flags of the World*, Emmering, Amsterdam, 1966.

Simmel, Georg, *Conflict*, tr. Kurt H. Wolff, Free Press, Glencoe, Ill., l9SS.

Slim, William, *Unofficial History*, Corgi Books, London, 1970.

Smith, Sydney, *Wings Day*, Collins, London, 1968.

Smyth, Sir John, *The Victoria Cross*, Muller, London, 1965.

Spencer, Herbert, *The Principles of Economy*, Appleton, New York, 1897.

Ssu-ma Ch'ien, *Shih Ji (Records of the Grand Historian of China)*, tr. Burton Watson, Columbia University Press, New York and London, 1961.

Steinberg, Jonathan, *Yesterday Deterrent*, Macdonald, London, 1965.

Storry, Richard, *A History of Modern Japan*, Penguin, London, 1960.

Stouffer, S. A., *et al.*, *The American Soldier*, Princeton University Press, Princeton, 1949.

Suetonius, *The Twelve Caesars*, tr. Robert Graves, Penguin, London, 1957.

Sun Tzu, *The Art of War*; see T. R. Phillips, *Roots of Strategy*.

Tacitus, *Histories*, tr. Kenneth Wellesley, Penguin, London, 1964.

"Tactician," *Tactics for Field Officers and Company Commanders of the New Armies*, Groom, London, 1916.

———, *The Battalion in Attack*, Groom, London, 1916.

Taylor, A. J. P., *The First World War*, Penguin, London, 1966.

Thomas, D. Winton (ed.), *Documents from Old Testament Times*, Nelson, London, 1958.

Thucydides, *History of the Peloponnesian War*, tr. Rex Warner, Penguin, London, 1954.

Tolkien, J. R. R., *The Hobbit*, Allen & Unwin, London, 1970 (19th imprint).

Tolstoy, Leo, *War and Peace*, tr. Rosemary Edmonds, Penguin, London, 1968.

Toynbee, Arnold J., *War and Civilization*, Oxford University Press, Oxford, 1951.

U.S. Army, *Drills and Ceremonies*, Department of the Army, FM 22-5, Washington, 1953.

———, *Infantry Drill Regulations*, Department of the Army, FM 22-5, Washington, 1941.

U.S. Government, *The Selective Service Regulations*, Department of State and Public Institutions, Washington, 1948.

U.S. Congress, *Hearings Before the Joint Committee on the Pearl Harbor Attack*, Washington, 1946.

Uxküll, Boris, *Arms and The Woman*, The Diaries of Baron Boris Uxküll,

1812-1819, ed. Delter von Uexküll, tr. Joel Carmichael, Secker & Warburg, London, 1966.

Vattel, Emmerich de, *The Law of Nations*, tr. Joseph Chitty, Sweet, Stevens & Maxwell, London, 1834.

Veblen, Thorstein, *The Theory of Business Enterprise*, Scribner's, New York, 1932.

Vegetius, *The Military Institutions of the Romans*, tr. John Clarke; see T. R. Phillips, *Roots of Strategy*.

Viereck, G. S., *Spreading Germs of Hate*, Duckworth, London, 1931.

Vischer, A. L., *Barbed Wire Disease*, tr. S. A. Kinnier Wilson, Bale, London, 1919.

Voughan, Charles Richard, *Narrative of the Siege of Zaragoza*, Ridgway, London, 1836.

Waley, Arthur, *The Secret History of the Mongols*, Allen & Unwin, London, 1963.

Walker, T. J., *The Depôt for Prisoners of War at Norman Cross*, Constable, London, 1915.

War Office, *Ceremonial*, H.M.S.O., London, 1962.

——, *Field Service Regulation* (41461), H.M.S.O., London, 1905.

——, *Instructions to Military Cooks* (40185/2364), H.M.S.O., London, 1878.

——, *Manual of Military Cooking* (103/Misc/933), H.M.S.O., London 1918.

——, *Musketry Regulations* (7754), H.M.S.O., London, 1910.

——, *Small Arms Training* (50498/187-7), H.M.S.O., London, 1924.

——, *Statistical Report on the Health of the Army 1943-45*, H.M.S.O., London, 1948.

Weber, Max, *Essays in Sociology*, tr. H. H. Gerth and C. Wright Mills, Routledge & Kegan Paul, London, 1948.

Williams, Eric, *The Wooden Horse*, Collins, London, 1949.

Wilson, Andrew, *War Gaming*, Penguin, London, 1970.

Woetzel, Robert K., *The Nuremberg Trials in International Law*, Stevens, London, 1960.

Wolfenstein, Martha, *Disaster*, Routledge & Kegan Paul, London, 1957.

Wolfkill, Grant, *Reported to be Alive*, Simon & Schuster, New York, 1965.

Woodham-Smith, Cecil, *The Reason Why*, Penguin, London, 1958.

Xenophon, *A History of My Times*, tr. Rex Warner, Penguin, London, 1966.

——, *The Persian Expedition*, tr. Rex Warner, Penguin, London, 1949.

——, *Memoirs of Socrates and the Symposium*, tr. Hugh Tredennick, Penguin, London, 1970.

Zhukov, Georgi K., *Marshal Zhukov's Greatest Battles*, Macdonald, London, 1969.

Zinn, Howard, *Vietnam - The Logic of Withdrawal*, Beacon Press, Boston, 1967.